MORE SKILFUL SOCCER

In this book I want to emphasize the positive, attacking aspects of soccer, and above all, I want to concentrate on skill. It is easy to become suffocated in systems and tactics, but more important is playing skill and all young players should strive to develop this from the start. Time and time again in the heat of international competition it has been skill that has separated the winners from the losers – the success of Argentina in the 1970 World Cup is a prime example. Today, modern managers are looking for skilful players more than ever before, and here, in this book, I am suggesting various ways and means of improving your game. For the illustrated practice routines, that fine player Martin Dobson of Everton and Burnley, is shown in numerous action sequences photographed specially for the book. In addition, further practice sessions are illustrated in which various moves and counter-moves are analysed; for these, the Shrewsbury Town goalkeeper Ken Mulhearn lent his services. Finally, in a section called 'Learning from the Professionals' we look at the particular skills of a number of top international players and discuss their techniques and ability. The object of the book is to encourage all young players to work at basic skills which are the key to success in soccer.

MORE SKILFUL SOCCER

by

Robin Trimby

LONDON
VICTOR GOLLANCZ LTD
in association with Peter Crawley
1980

ISBN 0 575 02718 5

Printed in Great Britain by
W. S. Cowell Ltd, Ipswich, Suffolk

CONTENTS

ACKNOWLEDGEMENTS

The author would like to thank the Press Association, Associated Press, Sportsfoto Metelmann and Camera Press Ltd for their permission to reproduce photographs, Peter Langmead for his photographs of Martin Dobson and John Rea for his of Ken Mulhearn. I also wish to thank Everton FC and Shrewsbury Town FC for their co-operation and to acknowledge the assistance of the young footballers of Shrewsbury School who have enthusiastically helped to illustrate the book. Finally I am indebted to Margaret Alston without whom my handwriting would never have been translated into legible type.

R.W.T.

FOREWORD

by Alan Durban

Manager of Stoke City Football Club

More Skilful Soccer is another rewarding publication by Robin Trimby. It will appeal mainly to the younger player whether his future interests are at amateur or professional level. In many books of this nature writers have made the grave error of bypassing the basic skills of soccer, but fortunately this book highlights the need for all players to recognize the importance of acquiring good basic techniques. Natural ball players are blessed with many of these skills but even they can acquire new ideas and become more tactically aware by reading this book.

The author confirms my belief in the essential need for more small-sided practice games. He also suggests several excellent ways of improving your heading, kicking, trapping, dribbling and tackling. The photographs are extremely well presented, giving the reader the chance to compare professionals with schoolboys and to note amongst other things, how much shorter the professional's stride appears, giving the player better balance in order to tackle, sprint or change direction.

I found, as no doubt you will, that the 'question and answer' chapter is fascinating. I was pleased with my 85 per cent success but my defensive positions were never too impressive in my playing days, and the answers only confirmed this. Finally Robin Trimby reminds the young footballer how much he can learn from the professionals and I am delighted to see his choice of such skilful players who have so much to offer. But football is a simple game, genius is simplicity. Good players make difficult things look easy and such a book as this will certainly help you raise your standards. May it raise them beyond your wildest dreams.

INTRODUCTION

Normal life in Argentina came to a complete halt in 1978; thousands of West Germans cheered themselves hoarse in 1974; the Brazilians turned Mexico into their own particular fiesta in 1970 and which Englishmen will ever forget Wembley in 1966? Yes, the World Cup confirms soccer as the most popular team game in the world, thousands of people play it and millions more watch it. Naturally enough an increasing amount is written about football, more is televised and thus more is discussed and argued than ever before. All this is splendid in many ways, but it brings with it two real threats to the game itself; firstly in the passionate but blind spectators who support one team at the expense of everything else; and secondly in the theories and tactics of coaches who become bogged down in 'Systems' and turn a simple game into a complicated one. Both these supporters and these coaches are too often plagued by a fear of losing – and it is this fear which can tend to make soccer a negative, defensive game.

In this book I want to emphasize the positive, attacking aspects of soccer and, above all, I want to concentrate on skill. It was heartening to hear the England Team Manager, Ron Greenwood, state emphatically that young players should learn to play by improving their skill and not become suffocated by systems and tactics too early. It was equally rewarding to see how skill shone through the blanket defences and the tight marking of the World Cup in Argentina, in such players as Kempes and Rossi; and to find that the two outstanding attacking teams in the competition – Holland and Argentina – reached the final. Obviously few of us can hope to reach such heights.

However, better players who gain more enjoyment from the game of football are those who aim to improve their skills. Countless books and magazines give you all the information you require regarding your team or your favourite player, but very few concentrate on helping your own technique as a footballer; and in the following pages I shall be suggesting the main ways in which you can improve your own technique and your understanding of the game. Whatever your ability, whether you are in your school team or not, my advice is aimed at you. We do not all kick, head or trap a football in exactly the same manner, but there are certain fundamentals that every aspiring footballer must learn. I have concentrated on each of the basic skills in turn – kicking, trapping, dribbling, heading, tackling and goalkeeping – and have illustrated each with photographs of professionals, Martin Dobson of Everton and Burnley and Ken Mulhearn of Manchester City and Shrewsbury Town showing us what we should aim at; and other photographs of 15–17-year-old schoolboys demonstrating the same skills (not always with 100 per cent success) and reminding you that it is possible, with practice, for you to reach these standards during the coming years. You will note too, that where possible the players have been photographed performing such skills as heading, trapping and shooting under pressure (either being challenged or in a match situation). It is all too easy for a defender to trap a ball or for a goalkeeper to make a save without any challenge – but most unnatural, and we should always aim to connect our practices as closely as possible to what actually happens in a game. The best opportunity to test your personal skills lies in small-sided games (5-a-side, 4-a-side, etc) and these can, of course, be organized or remain completely unofficial, but, as I shall emphasize in the following chapters, you will also need to practise and improve your skills and technique on your own.

Once you can control the ball, kick and head properly, screen and dribble at the right moments then, and only then, is the time to bother yourself with systems and tactics. However, I have included a chapter on 'Learning from the Coach', in which I shall briefly explain the different team systems, and another 'Question and Answer' chapter which I have called 'Applying Skill in the Game'.

In this section, with the help of diagrams, I shall put you on the spot and ask you to imagine yourself in a game, having to make a rapid decision and applying your skill. Finally I include a chapter on 'Learning from the Professionals' as a reminder that you can learn a lot by watching the experts intelligently – a point too often neglected by those blinkered supporters who only wish to see their team win at any cost.

But do remember that my advice will be of little lasting value if you just read the book, look at the photographs and do no more. You may never find yourself playing in the World Cup Finals, but you will discover more fun in playing your own football and more rewards in watching it if you are prepared to practise hard and improve your skills.

CHAPTER 1
Kicking

The game of football is based on kicking and unless you learn to kick the ball properly with either foot you will never progress far. Sometimes when I watch a competitive match, at professional or club level, I wonder why the game is not called 'Headball', so often is the ball in the air and so monotonously do players keep lobbing the ball into the goalmouth, or punting the ball high up the field simply to clear it as quickly as possible. This is hardly football and the intelligent, successful teams keep the ball on the ground as often as they can, using the chip or the lob as an occasional variation. Thus the art of kicking is a vital fundamental in football.

There are many ways in which a ball can be kicked, but I shall consider them under six separate headings: the side-footed pass, the instep drive, the chip (and the lob), the bent pass, the volley (and half-volley) and finally other types of kick. With the help of photographs of Martin Dobson I shall first explain the basic technique involved in kicking a football and then at the end of the chapter, I shall suggest various practice routines which will improve your kicking skills. It is worth remembering that the great footballing stars we so admire and whose autographs we clamour for, have all had to work hard and long behind the scenes, practising their technique and improving their skill. Do not for a moment imagine that Rivelino's explosive left foot or Beckenbauer's cultured right foot developed 'naturally' – a great deal of conscientious and dedicated kicking practice has taken place; and the earlier you start practising the better.

When you watch Kevin Keegan pushing a short pass, or Trevor Brooking spraying a long one, whether you admire Krol's smooth distribution or Bettega's deadly volleying, Brady's immaculate chipping or Dalglish's ruthless shooting there are three principles which all these great players will be following:

(a) Always keep your eye on the ball.
(b) Position the non-kicking foot correctly.
(c) Ensure that you are properly balanced.

Simple enough on paper, yet how often do you take your eye off the ball for that vital second as a challenger moves in; how many times do you put the ball over the bar simply because your non-kicking foot is placed too far away from the ball; and how often do you fail to kick accurately because you are unbalanced at the moment of contact?

Finally, before we look more closely at the different types of kick, remember the importance at first, of concentrating on accuracy rather than power in your kicking. The strength will come later; the technique must be right from the beginning.

KICKING WITH THE SIDE OF THE FOOT

We often need to play the short (5–10 metre) pass in football whether backwards, sideways or forwards and the most accurate – and thus the most common – type of kick used, is the side-footed one demon-

1 Here we see the first stage of the short side-footed pass. Notice the position of the left foot alongside the ball and see how the right knee leads the right foot into the kick.

2 The eyes are still focused on the ball; but note how the right foot has 'opened up' and is coming through square on to the target.

strated in photographs **1–3**. Notice how our professional has his eye on the ball, standing foot alongside it and, perhaps most important, the knee of his kicking foot over the ball in order to keep the pass low. The movement here is more of a stabbing motion often with a limited follow through and, of course, the same technique will apply if you are volleying a side-footed pass. Yet remember that even these short passes must be hit firmly as well as accurately.

Note, too, the way in which he is beautifully balanced when making the pass and the fact that his arms are very much part of this balance. Indeed, the use of the arms in football (fairly of course!) is often neglected and I maintain that I can spot a real young footballer from a distance by the way he uses his arms to balance himself.

KICKING WITH THE INSTEP

This is probably the most common way of kicking and can be used when passing or shooting, and played short, long, high or low. If you look at photographs **4–7** you will see the vital stages of the *low* instep pass clearly demonstrated. Notice the balance of the body, the head over the ball and the position of the left foot as close to the ball as possible, so that when the right foot comes through, the knee is over the top of the ball, thus ensuring the low driven pass we are looking for. Power and distance come partly through timing, but largely due to the backlift and follow through. As in golf, so in football they are both a crucial part of technique and you will note the full backlift in photograph **4** and equally the poised follow through in photograph **7**.

3 Finally the follow-through, giving the pass power as well as precision. Look at the perfect balance and the use of the arms to secure this.

4

5

6

4 The low driven pass with the instep. The standing foot must be close to the ball if we want to deliver a low pass.

5 The moment of contact. Look at the position of the head and the right knee particularly – both *over* the ball.

6 The follow-through for power – but look again at the head and the balance.

7 Further follow-through for that 30-metre blockbuster!

7

So far we have only considered the *low* driven pass, but equally important is the lofted driven pass. When you are aiming to switch play from one wing to another with a crossfield ball, or clearing from defence to one of your forwards, or perhaps seeking to centre the ball to your tall centre forward at the far post, you will find the lofted drive (or possibly the chip which I will deal with in the next section) far more effective than trying to thread a low pass through a crowd of players. All the principles attached to the low driven pass apply again in the lofted pass, *except* that the non-kicking foot should be

9

10

11

8 Moving in at an angle to deliver a lofted, driven pass. Look at Martin Dobson's intense concentration which is a special feature of this sequence.

9 Notice how he has given himself more space here, by placing the standing foot a little wider and a little behind the ball.

10 The moment of contact. Note the snap-like action of the knee as the foot comes through *under* the ball.

11 The follow-through with the kicking leg coming across the body. Compare this with photograph **7**.

placed *behind* and wide of the ball as in photograph **9**, enabling our player to lean backwards rather than forwards. Compare the angle of the body in photographs **9** and **4** and remember, too, that you will often find that you can gain an extra 10–15 metres if you run diagonally at the ball rather than directly behind it. Goalkeepers should make a particular note of this point.

It is often easier to gain greater power when driving a *moving* ball, but more difficult to retain accuracy and when you are practising your kicking it is important to practise with this in mind. At all events, check your technique with a stationary ball first and then move on to more relevant practices as soon as possible.

THE CHIP AND THE LOB

These are also passes in which the instep is generally used, but many people tend to confuse these lofted kicks and forget that there is a real difference between them. Firstly the chip. This is demonstrated quite clearly in photographs **12-15** and is often used instead of a lofted driven pass. The difference must be realized however. A lofted driven pass can achieve greater distance, with the ball climbing and then dropping steadily in flight, while the chipped pass rises more steeply and falls more sharply too. In terms of technique the vital difference lies in the follow through; the chip has no proper follow through, aiming to impart back spin on the ball, while the lofted drive has a fuller follow through. You will see the difference if you

12 Here is the approach for a chip. You will notice that this has more in common with photograph **4** than photograph **8**.

13 The moment of contact as the foot cuts *under* the ball. But you will see the professional's standing foot quite close to the ball.

14 You can almost see the ball 'back-spinning' here as it starts to rise. Look too at the position of the player's head.

15 No real follow-through is needed when executing the chip, but notice how steeply the ball is rising.

compare photographs **11** and **15**. The lob, on the other hand is used more often on the volley than anything else, and is usually an intentional attempt at an 'up and under', used to prey upon the nerves of a suspect goalkeeper and an uncertain defence. The technique for the lob is similar to that of the lofted instep kick, but the follow through of the knee involves an upward movement.

THE VOLLEY AND HALF VOLLEY

One of the finest sights in football is the volleyed goal, cleanly hit and crisply timed; but the volley which clears a dangerous centre is just as important, and how often have we all seen the sliced volley with the weak foot which finishes up in our own goal! It is a difficult technique but if you study photographs **16** and **17** you will immediately see that the key to volleying downwards lies with the *knee being over the ball*. It is not so difficult to volley upwards, but only by bringing the knee over the ball will you keep the ball down; yet look also at the balance, the eyes and the pivoted motion in our photographs.

16 Martin Dobson executing a volley as he moves onto a driven centre. Notice the right knee *above* the ball.

17 The moment of impact – a cleanly struck volley. No wonder the goalkeeper looks concerned.

18 A schoolboy moving onto a volley. Note that he does not stand and wait for the ball to reach him, or he will be tackled by the closing defender.

19 Compare this volley with photograph **17**. A well-balanced attempt, but he is a little too far from the ball. . . .

20 . . . and as a result the ball flies just over the crossbar.

You might at first find it easier to stoop low and head the ball (although this can be dangerous) or, like so many less skilled players, let it bounce before kicking it; but if you can move towards the ball and meet it on the volley you will steal vital split seconds from your opponents, so get practising.

Likewise the half-volley requires timing and balance, and though used less frequently than the volley, the ball which is struck just as it hits the ground can travel very sweetly – as long as that knee of yours is still over the ball.

SWERVING OR BENDING THE BALL

Ten years ago very few players bothered to try to 'bend' the ball but the South Americans and the Continentals soon began to demonstrate the value of this swerving ball; and now many of the great players use the outside and the inside of their stronger foot more often than any part of their weaker one. Bending the ball has proved particularly effective at free kicks and corners and we saw some remarkable goals scored in this way in the 1978 World Cup. Bonhoff of West Germany is particularly worth watching in this respect, as is Dirceu of Brazil who 'bent' several amazing shots in Argentina.

The complete player learns to use both feet and it is not a bad idea to practise with a boot on your weak foot and a gym shoe or slipper on your good one but it often deceives your opponent if you suddenly flick the ball through with the outside of your stronger foot.

In photographs **21-23** you can see the ball being struck with the

21 A young player moves in to 'bend' the ball with the outside of his right foot. Notice how he is going to place the standing foot wide of the ball.

22 The moment of impact. A fine picture of the right foot coming 'across' the ball.

23 The follow-through – and note how the right foot has moved across the body. The ball is beginning to swerve here – and finished up with the goalkeeper diving to his left!

outside of the right foot and, with a follow-through slightly across the body, the ball will swerve to the right in flight, as it will when struck with the *inside* of the left foot. Reverse the procedure for the ball to swerve to the left and remember that the slower the ball is hit, the earlier it will swerve in flight.

Naturally it is essential to perfect the straight-forward types of kick, which we have already considered, before trying to swerve or bend the ball; but you only have to ask your goalkeeper's view to appreciate the potential danger of the shot that changes direction.

OTHER TYPES OF KICK

A football ground is not a circus ring and there is no profit in entertaining the crowd with a series of unusual skills when they do not contribute to your team's chances of winning the game. Yet there are moments in a game when the 'toe punt' is necessary and although we cannot control such a kick, it can take the opposing goalkeeper by surprise when we have to stretch to reach a half-chance.

Equally there are occasions when the *back-heeled pass* can switch play unexpectedly, leaving a colleague the space to move forward positively, but we must never forget that where possible *we should play the way we are facing* in football, and it is my belief that the back-heel is often used unnecessarily. In the same way the *bicycle kick* also tends to be used ambitiously when a more simple pass back to a supporting colleague frequently represents better tactics. However, when the bicycle kick is carried out with technical control it is an exciting and highly effective weapon. But do not try it until you have mastered the demanding skill required and even then I should not choose a hard surface for your experiment!

Practice Routines to Improve your Kicking

(a) Despite all the modern coaching books, and all the intricate practices, the best way for you to start to improve your technique is quite simply to find a wall of any description and to practise kicking a ball against it. The type of ball you use is irrelevant. It does not have to be a football, and a tennis ball or a similarly small ball provides the best practice of all. This is how many of the great players improve their control and their kicking and there are plenty of variations. You can have a contest between your right and left foot; count the number of times you strike a marked circle on the wall. Why not chalk in several circles, with a bull's eye in the centre offering additional points and see what you can score in twenty attempts? Start with a stationary ball but then try to take the rebound first time. There are endless possibilities and you are not only having fun, you are improving your kicking technique too, including some volleying and half-volleying. Two final words of warning however. *Never* use your hands in these private contests and mind the windows!

(b) If you are in a group or team practice try the following: place one (or two) balls on the centre spot as a target and line up two opposing teams along the penalty lines, one facing the other, with as many balls as possible allotted to each team. The aim is to drive the target ball towards and finally over the opponent's penalty line by striking it with a series of firm, low passes. Although this particular contest often ends in a goalless draw it calls for calmness under pressure and real accuracy in the low driven kick.

(c) You can practise chipping on your own – and bending the ball too – by using the wall again if it is high enough. But as you improve, try chipping at the crossbar from the edge of the penalty area and see how many direct hits you achieve in ten attempts. If you can find a partner to compete against, so much the better and do not forget to practise chipping with the weaker foot as well.

(d) As you begin to master the basic techniques of kicking – but not before – why not practise bending and swerving the ball? After all the Brazilians are doing so almost as soon as they can walk. Start on your own against the wall, and then place any small, sturdy object in a direct line between you and the wall, aiming to bend the ball round it. Alternatively place a corner flag on the penalty spot and another in the centre of the goal and see how often you can swerve the ball around the first flag and into the opposite half of the goal. It is not easy – even without a goalkeeper – but well worth mastering.

(e) Finally, if you have three friends or you are in a team practice, try placing a corner flag (later 3 or 4) in the centre of a circle of 20 metres diameter. Split into two pairs, facing each other and try to bend the ball round the flags to your partner. A point every time you find your colleague without his having to move; but remember to practise swerving the ball with the outside *and* the inside of the foot.

CHAPTER 2

Trapping and Control

It is no good learning to kick properly until you can bring the ball under control and, as we have seen from the practices at the end of the last chapter, the two skills are inseparably mixed.

When we watch the professional player controlling a difficult pass do we not sometimes feel that he must have the ball on some invisible string, so well does he take possession of it – with his feet, thighs, chest or head? Yet how often do we find that simple pass bouncing away from us as we attempt to control, trap or 'kill' the ball. Next time you watch a match, notice how the great players give themselves an additional few inches of space, by bringing the ball under instant control. Remember that the more quickly we can control the ball, the more chance we have of passing it accurately before we are tackled.

So let us look closely as the various methods of trapping and control and at the technique involved, remembering that in all forms of stationary trapping it is essential that whichever part of the body you are using – head, foot, chest or thigh – must 'give' a little, to cushion the ball just as it is about to make contact.

CONTROL WITH THE FOOT

There are numerous ways of controlling the ball with the foot and when you receive any ground pass from your own team you will need to cushion the ball at your feet. But the first trap that you should perfect is the simple 'squeeze' trap which involves controlling the ball between your foot and the ground, using either the sole or the side of the boot.

24 Although marked tightly, Martin Dobson waits to control this high ball from his defence.

26 Notice here how well our player uses his body to 'screen' the ball as he waits for support to arrive.

25 The moment of trapping with the inside of the foot. See how he is already moving left and yet how tightly he has controlled the ball.

27 Again the tight marker and the ball waiting to be controlled, but note how, this time, Martin Dobson is starting to move to his right.

28 The moment of trapping with the outside of the foot. Note the balanced position and the right knee over the ball here.

29 On the move, with the ball perfectly controlled and the body preventing a tackle from behind.

Once you have conquered this, try trapping the ball on the move, again squeezing it between your foot and the ground, but dragging it to your left or right as you bring it under control. Look at our professional in photographs **24-29** and note how quickly he is on the move with the ball tightly under control and in position to shake off any opponent who might be moving in to tackle. Try trapping with the outside of your foot as well as the inside. You might not find this easy at first but it will help you to move off in either direction and thus make life far more difficult for the player marking you. Martin Dobson gives us a perfect illustration of these skills in photographs **24-29**. Trapping the ball with the inside and then with the outside of the foot, notice how he still shields the ball as he controls it, while his concentration and balance are an object lesson to all young foot-

[25]

30 A young player concentrating on the dropping ball. He does not look entirely confident, but he *is* moving towards it.

31 The trap itself and quite well executed considering the expectant defender close at hand. But compare the technique with photograph **28**.

ballers. In photographs **30** and **31** we see a young footballer attempting the same skill under pressure. He has made a creditable attempt without quite the poise of our professional.

Often in a game, you will find the ball coming towards you at that difficult knee height and (unless you try to volley it first time) the most effective method of control is to cushion it with the inside of your foot as in photograph **32**. Whether it be a bouncing ball on a hard pitch or a low driven ball from friend or foe, Martin Dobson shows us exactly how to bring it down and under control in the quickest possible manner. When you feel that you have begun to master these techniques why not attempt the instep trap? This is

32 Cushioning a lofted pass. An important technique to conquer and not always quite as easy as it is made to look here.

33 The 'concave' trap. A young player here hollowing his chest and rounding his arms to allow the ball to drop from his chest to his feet. Notice the good, close defensive marking too.

34 The 'convex' trap – Martin Dobson cushioning the ball as he thrusts his chest forward. Compare with photograph **33**.

occasionally used to pull down a high dropping ball and depends upon your catching and cradling the ball in your instep before it drops to the ground. The cushioning effect is crucial here and this is a very difficult skill. I certainly would not recommend it in your own penalty area, but it is well worth practising.

CONTROL WITH THE CHEST

As we have seen the ball often spends far too much of its time in the air and we frequently have to control it with other parts of our anatomy than the foot. I once saw a particularly talented player, when his side were comfortably on top, trap the ball (intentionally) with his backside by gently squatting on it as it hit the ground! I do not recommend that, but control with the head, the chest and the thigh are essential to the ambitious young footballer.

There are two equally effective methods of controlling the ball with your chest, either by the concave trap (photograph **33**) or as shown in photograph **34** by the convex trap. In the first instance the chest is hollowed and the body stoops forward; but in the more common convex trap note how the chest is thrust out more obviously and how the arms almost welcome the ball in. However, in both instances the arms and eyes are again important and the cushioning effect is vital.

CONTROL WITH THE HEAD AND THE THIGH

Finally as you become more confident in your control, try trapping the ball on the thigh (as in photograph **35**) or on the head. These methods of control are normally used when faced with dropping balls and both require careful timing together with a pronounced cushioning effect. In photographs **36–38** you will see our professional combining several of these skills – cushioning the ball on his head in **36**, then on his thigh and finally half volleying a pass to one of his forwards. Look at the calm poise and control, even though he is challenged. In a match you will not often have to control the ball with your thigh and very rarely with your head; but they are both worth adding to your repertoire. If you can really work upon all these methods of trapping and control and master the different techniques, you will soon be able to receive a ball from any angle at any height with complete confidence. But it will take a lot of practice!

35 A fine photograph of the thigh trap. Look at the balance and control here as the ball is cushioned on the thigh. So securely is it 'killed' that it almost looks as if the player is holding it in place with his hand.

36 Cushioning the ball on the head. Notice how the knees and the body have 'given' a little at the moment of contact.

37 From head to thigh.

38 From thigh to foot, and our player half-volleys a short pass to a waiting colleague.

Practice Routines to Improve your Control

(a) We have already seen how, by kicking a ball against a wall, we can improve our control and any practice involving kicking will inevitably assist trapping as well. To give yourself some competition, draw a circle on the ground – fairly large at first, if you like – and set up a number of skittles around the circle. Throw the ball in the air or against the wall and try to control it without disturbing the skittles. Keep a count of your score and then come back and beat your record another day.

(b) Yet the most valuable basic practice of trapping techniques is to be found in the company of one or two other players. Throwing the ball to each other at various heights, controlling it and returning it. Having improved your own control without any opponents to bother about, then try to put yourself into a match situation. It is important to remember that it is all very well controlling the ball perfectly in our own back yard with nobody else around; but we have to 'kill the ball dead' in a match when opponents are threatening, colleagues are waiting hopefully and spectators are shouting. So, as with all practices, try to put yourself into a realistic match situation, as soon as you have mastered those fundamental techniques on your own.

(c) Mark out a square (large at first but smaller as you improve) or use a 'grid' and work with two other players. A throws the ball to C who controls it and moves as B, starting alongside A, comes in to challenge. C then plays the ball back to A who has found a support position, still within the boundary of the square of course. Vary the service, keep changing round and your control in tight situations will improve rapidly.

CHAPTER 3

Heading

Whether we like it or not the ball is often in the air and if you look back at the 1978 World Cup or watch any English, European or American League game, you will realize that almost as many goals are scored with the head as with the feet. Indeed, central defenders and central strikers sometimes head the ball as often as they kick it during a match. It is therefore vital that you learn to head correctly as soon as possible. Obviously the younger you are, the less power you will impart when heading the ball, but if your technique is correct then you need not worry – the strength will develop later. Equally you must not despair just because you are smaller than your opponents. There are many outstanding headers of the ball who are not six-footers, Keegan and Bettega amongst them; and the secret is one of timing and jumping rather than mere height.

However, before we consider jumping, timing and challenging you must first make absolutely sure that you head the ball properly. The basic principles of heading are quite clear:

(a) Eyes on the ball always.

(b) Use the forehead (you will soon realize that the remainder of your head does not approve of the hard thud of a football).

(c) Head from the hips, *not* just by waggling the head itself. Power stems from the waist and from the legs.

(d) Time your spring when jumping to head.

If you look at the sequence of photographs **39-43** showing our professional heading the ball, you will see these points stylishly underlined. But remember that in a game you will very rarely be given the chance to stand still and head the ball; you will almost certainly be challenged in the air and the timing of your jump will be crucial. It is also important to note that the defensive header requires a rather different technique from the attacking one. Photographs **39-45** should be compared with **46-48**.

If you are a forward you should look with particular care at photographs **39-45** for it is far more difficult to head downwards and far more difficult for a goalkeeper to stop a ball headed at his feet rather than his hands. See how our professional has got above the ball and punched it downwards. Look especially at the follow-through in

39 40

39 The attacking header. As Martin Dobson comes to meet the ball notice how he starts to wind himself up.

40 Fully coiled and about to strike. Look at the arms and head here – and at the height he has jumped.

41 The attacking header just after the moment of contact. See how the neck, arms and upper body have now un-coiled to give additional power.

41

42 The attacking header being struck downwards. Look at the follow-through of the neck and forehead.

43 What any forward hopes to see, as the opposing goalkeeper dives in vain.

44 Here we see a schoolboy attempting a header at goal. He is timing his jump quite well as he meets a centre from the left. Compare with photograph **39**.

45 Just after the moment of impact. Notice the swivel of the hips and the neck, together with the follow-through of the forehead, but compare with photograph **41**.

photographs **41** and **42**, but notice too the body turning from the hips not just from the neck. Then compare your own technique with that of the young forward in photographs **44** and **45**. Most headers involve a turning of the hips and a change of direction for the ball, particularly when we are heading a centre from the wing, whether we be forwards or defenders and you must remember this in practice.

In photographs **46–48** we see the ball being headed *upwards* and away out of danger. No defender worth his salt is going to head the ball downwards, unless he is unmarked in midfield or has moved into the opposing penalty area to try to score himself. Indeed, you may well have seen your favourite centre half heading the ball clear almost as far as you can kick it! It is all a matter of technique and if you can model yourself on our expert or take heart from the schoolboy header in photograph **48** you will not go far wrong.

There are, in addition, the flicked and glancing headers and the backward header which the best players use skilfully, but these still involve the same techniques – eye on the ball, use of the forehead, the last minute pivot from the hips and the follow-through.

46 The defensive header – just after the moment of impact. Look particularly at the way the neck and chest have thrust forward in the follow-through and how the ball has been headed safely upwards and away from danger.

47 The defensive header by a schoolboy. He has done well to win this centre against a strong challenge. Notice that he has timed his jump correctly and used his arms and body to impart additional power into the clearance.

48 A fine picture of a typical defensive header. You can see how, despite the attacker's challenge, our centre half has jumped well, used his body excellently (look at those arms) and followed-through with his eyes as well as his forehead.

Practice Routines to Improve
your Heading

(a) Start against that wall again, simply heading the rebound back for as many successive headers as possible. This will help you to use the forehead correctly, to punch the ball from the hips and to strengthen your neck muscles. Initially in this and any heading practice a lightweight ball should be used and there is no need to practise heading with a proper football until you are 14 or 15.

(b) With your friend, throw the ball to each other heading it in return. Do not stand too far apart at first (3 or 4 metres will do) and concentrate on punching the ball downwards at your partner's knees. The server should then aim just above the head so that the receiver has to jump, yet still tries to return the header downwards. Finally extend this into a threesome so that you are starting to practise the sideways header and the pivot from the hips – yet it is still important to keep the triangle fairly small.

(c) If you or your team have a sports hall or gymnasium nearby use a volleyball court (a shortened tennis court or an improvised area in your back garden will do) for Head Tennis. This can be valuable, competitive practice for your heading, particularly if the two teams place defenders at the back of the court so that they head upwards for length and power and attackers close to the net to head downwards. A properly organized game of Head Tennis is great fun, too.

(d) When you have improved your heading technique in these ways you should be ready for a more challenging practice. Easily the best I have come across involves two teams (6–8 players each is ideal), playing across the width of the penalty area. Each team scores by heading the ball over the opponent's penalty line. The contest starts with both teams lined up facing their opponents' half and jumping to head. Only when the ball drops to waist height or goes outside the penalty area may hands be used and then the ball must be headed on to a colleague and never thrown. Fierce competition often develops and you will soon learn how to head under challenge. ·

[35]

CHAPTER 4

Dribbling

Ten years ago when wingers seemed to be disappearing from the game of football, it looked as if the days of the great dribblers were over. But in recent years the individual genius has fortunately returned to the touchlines and dribblers such as Robertson of Scotland, Barnes and Cunningham of England, James of Wales and George Best of Northern Ireland have recaptured the skills of the great Tom Finney and Stanley Matthews of past decades; and who can forget the close ball control and exciting acceleration of the Argentinian forwards in the 1978 World Cup series? Or the magic of Cruyff?

Nowadays, of course, it is not just the winger or the forward who possesses dribbling skill, and defenders can be most effective bursting through from the back with the ball at their feet. One of the overriding lessons of the 1978 World Cup series came from the Dutch and their concept of 'total football'. There seemed no set pattern of defenders and forwards, numbers meant little; and we saw full backs like Brandt, centre backs like Krol bursting forward to make and score goals; while forwards like Van der Kerkhof and Hahn dropped back and did the defender's job. If you have the ability to dribble you can be a key member of your team and, whatever your position on the field, your contribution will be increased if you can take opposing players on. It is worth remembering how many goals are made by players reaching the opposing goal line, before pulling the ball back. How do we get players to the goal line? Either by a through pass, which a good defence should block, or by a dribble, which is much more difficult to stop. So what distinguishes the dribbler?

(a) Ball control (close control while on the move).
(b) Change of speed (the ability to dribble slowly at a defender and then to accelerate past him).
(c) The ability to dodge, swerve and turn (which relies of course on our being perfectly balanced as we approach our opponent).
(d) A natural feint (each dribbler has his own brand; but whether yours is a shrug of the shoulders, or a shuffle of the feet, you must aim to send your opponent the wrong way, to sell him the dummy!).

Martin Dobson shows us all these qualities in this dribbling sequence. In photograph **49** he drags the defender one way; in **50** he uses the outside of his foot to change direction. With the opponent off balance he accelerates past him in photograph **51** and yet still retains balance and control in **52**. Compare this with our schoolboy dribbling past a

49 Dribbling   our player is taking the ball as close as he possibly can to the defender, pulling him slightly towards the camera, with the inside of his right foot.

50 Having wrong-footed his opponent, the attacker now moves to his right. Note his perfect balance here as he switches the ball to the outside of his right foot.

51 Then the quick acceleration as the attacker sees the gap, while the defender tries to recover his balance.

52 Still perfectly in control of the ball with the defender floundering.

53 A young forward running at opponent. At this stage the expectant defender is not sure what will happen next.

54 A well-balanced action shot of our schoolboy changing direction. Compare this with photograph **50**.

55 Going for the gap with the defender wrong-footed – compare with photograph **51**.

defender in photographs **53-55** and you will realize that you can learn to dribble at any age.

The Johann Cruyffs are, of course, born not made but if you have a natural feint and a change of speed, develop it, practise your dribbling. Yet never forget that, although a dribbler often catches the eye, he can hold on to the ball too long – and a quick accurate pass is often better than all the dribbling in the world.

Practice Routines to Improve your Dribbling

In all your practices start by dribbling with a slightly under-inflated ball, the lighter and livelier the ball the more difficult it is to control. But the sooner you can dribble with a tennis ball the quicker your skill will improve.

(a) The long established routine of dribbling in and out of sticks remains the best starting practice on your own and you can easily time yourself against the clock, first with a large ball and then, later on, a smaller one. Gradually reduce the distance between the posts too.

(b) After you have mastered the sticks, gather some of your pals together with a ball each and construct a circle about the size of the centre circle. Then start dribbling your ball inside it while at the same time avoiding all others. Keep on the move, but change pace, change direction, dribble with the left foot, then with the right and at all times retain tight control of your ball inside the circle. You will find that this is all valuable dribbling practice, with others close at hand, but you will gain even more if you can do all this *with your head up*.

(c) The best dribbling practice against an opponent is really in the game itself, but if you can persuade young brother or father to act as a defender in the garden or on the beach, always try to ensure that you dribble at them in a confined space and do not forget that it is crucial to take the ball as close as possible to your opponent (even Dad!) before trying to go past him.

In all these practices remember to concentrate on your change of speed and your balance while ensuring that the ball is under tight close control as you lure your opponent.

Screening

When we dribble the ball, we ought automatically to use our body in acting as a barrier between the ball and our opponent. This is called 'screening' and this is a technique which we should, for a moment, consider because it is closely connected with ball control and dribbling. The Continentals and South Americans still tend to screen the ball more naturally than we do, and I shall never forget my first amateur international for England, in Luxembourg, when moving in to challenge one of our opponents, I found that he simply stopped the ball dead, ran round it so that he was facing his own goal and thrust his rather large posterior between me and the ball! I was rather taken aback but he was, of course, only taking the art of screening the ball to extremes.

If you watch the top players closely you will notice how naturally they keep their body between the ball and the opponent. Here in photographs **56** and **57** we see a young professional holding off a determined tackle by Martin Dobson. Note how he uses his arms and

56 Screening. The young player in white is holding off a fierce challenge from behind; but notice how the ball is kept well away from the opponent yet still under control. Note too the vital use of the arms in screening.

57 Another method of screening with the ball here being controlled by the underneath of the boot. Look, too, at the physical contact inevitable in this sort of situation. Defenders should study the good challenging position.

58 Here a schoolboy screens the ball with the outside of his right foot and there is no way (without fouling) that the defender can tackle.

59 Again the arms are important here, but so is the close control. Compare with photograph **57**.

60 This is what will happen if you do not screen the ball properly. Our young forward has shown the defender too much of the ball and a firm decisive tackle is the result.

61 This is a good example of a sliding tackle; notice how the challenger has his eyes on the ball throughout this sequence.

his body to screen the ball and how he uses the outside of his foot to keep control until support arrives. Then compare this technique with photographs **58–61** of schoolboys screening and tackling. There are valuable lessons here for defenders and attackers. If you can use your body to protect the ball in this way you will retain possession for much longer, even if you have to pass backwards in the end.

Practice Routines to Improve your Screening

Screening practices are inevitably involved in dribbling ones, but try dribbling the ball against an imaginary opponent, constantly changing the position of your body in order to protect the ball. You can use trees or posts to act as these imaginary defenders or, even better, if you possess a lively dog, try screening the ball from him – and watch your ankles! Then find yourself an opponent, mark out a square (or a 'grid') and see how long you can retain possession by dribbling and screening within the confined area. Splendid practice for both the screener and the tackler.

Finally look again at the poise and control of our professional as he goes past a defender in photographs **49–52** and do not forget the years of dedicated practice that have led to such exciting skill.

[41]

CHAPTER 5

Tackling

We have so far looked at the skills and techniques which are the foundation for attacking football. Ball control, shooting, heading and dribbling all involve positive, creative skills. Yet before we can show our ability with the ball we have to win it first. For all the emphasis in this book on improving your skill, you must never forget that football *is* a physical game and all the elegant ball control in the world is of little value unless you are prepared to meet a tackle determinedly, challenge courageously and accept the knocks and bruises which are all part of the game. Not only does it disrupt the flow of a game if you writhe on the ground after taking a hard knock, it also makes it quite clear to your opponents that you will not be too happy with the next firm challenge. Naturally if you are badly injured, it is a different matter, but the dramatic acting and the hypocrisy of many of the professionals in this respect is one of the lessons to avoid.

Increasingly in modern football you will discover that players are coached to 'hold off' the tackle, to back away from the opponent with the ball, so that other defenders can recover. This is often good tactics. But this does *not* mean that tackling is a disappearing skill. Far from it – it remains a vital one, especially for defenders and especially in and around our own penalty box. Indeed, nowadays when forwards are frequently expected to interchange with defenders, it is even more important that you attacking players also learn how to tackle. In my experience as a coach, forwards are notoriously weak at tackling and how often have you seen even professional games won and lost due to a mistake by a forward trying to defend in his own penalty area. So whether you be a centre forward or a centre half take careful note of these reminders when tackling:

(a) Time your tackle. It is no good rushing at an opponent from several metres away. Move closer, as close as you possibly can and wait until he is off balance.

(b) Watch the ball and not your opponent's feet. Do not fall for the dummy or the fancy footwork.

(c) Ensure that your full weight goes into the tackle itself. Even if you are a lightweight you will be surprised how often you can dispossess a heavier opponent if you put your whole weight into the tackle.

(d) Attack the ball determinedly when you decide to tackle. It is no good dangling a foot vaguely in the direction of the opponent. You must tackle with the intention of winning the ball, so compete for it aggressively (though always fairly!).

62-64 *The block tackle.* Here we find the attacker with the ball and running at our defender just outside the penalty box. Remember not to rush into a tackle from too far away. As the forward loses control for a moment, the chance has come for our defender to move in decisively and win the ball. Note the weight which this young defender has imparted. It is important to get your shoulder into the tackle if possible and to keep your eyes on the ball as in this photograph. A fine example of a powerful tackle.

65-67 *The sliding tackle.* In this sequence the young forward is threatening to dribble past the defender's left side. Once again our challenger has closed on his opponent before putting in the tackle, and when the sliding tackle is made, although the defender does not immediately seem to have won the ball, he still has his weight coming through the ball and his eyes firmly on it.

Naturally you will tackle according to the precise situation and you can become a hero overnight with a last-ditch tackle on the goal-line; but there are two main ways of tackling:

TACKLING FROM THE FRONT

The Block Tackle, demonstrated in photographs **62–64**, is probably the most common method of tackling and you will notice how effectively the defender is about to bring his weight into the tackle. In this type of frontal tackle, your weight should be right over the ball and in our photograph the defender's shoulder will help ensure that this is so. Much will depend upon how fast you strike, but remember it is unlikely that the player with the ball will have such close control that his weight will be immediately over the ball as your challenge is made.

TACKLING FROM THE SIDE

If you are forced to challenge from the side – and this will particularly apply to the full back marking a tricky winger – then you are almost certainly going to have to make some form of sliding tackle. Many defenders prefer this tackle, especially on wet surfaces and if timed properly (as in photographs **60** and **61**) it can be most effective. However, it is worth remembering that if you fail to make contact with this tackle, you will be left stranded on the ground, while your opponent moves happily forward.

There are variations on this theme as seen in photographs **65–67**, but it is certainly possible to tackle from the side without sliding and finishing on your backside. But whichever tackle you are forced to use, do not forget to keep your eye on the ball, to strike decisively and to make sure you get the ball and not the man!

[44]

While we are talking of physical contact in football do not neglect the fair shoulder charge (shoulder to shoulder), a perfectly legal challenge which is often neglected nowadays and very effective if delivered while your ball playing opponent is just off balance.

Practice Routines to Improve your Tackling

Tackling practices can only be really organized in a competitive situation and the best way to improve your tackling is during a five- or six-a-side practice game.

(a) However, we have already seen the value to the dribbler and to the tackler of practising in a confined area, one against one. On an even more elementary basis if you and your opponent stand a metre away from each other with a ball in the middle and both (together) move in to 'wedge' the ball between you, trying to squeeze it through, this will help you to acquire the right technique of the block tackle – and to feel your weight going in over the ball.

(b) Having mastered the elementary technique, why not find a local pitch? Ask your friend to stand on the half way line with the ball at his feet and simply try to stop him dribbling past you. When you win possession, change places and start again. I warn you that this can be a tiring practice, but a very valuable one, for you can practise jockeying, closing on your opponent, forcing him onto your stronger tackling foot, slowing him down and finally deciding on your final strike. Equally the player with the ball can improve his screening and dribbling skills.

These practices will help your tackling, but you will soon want to ask your school teacher or your coach to set up a more competitive practice in a realistic situation.

[45]

CHAPTER 6

Goalkeeping

If you are a young goalkeeper I suggest that you would be foolish to close the door on other, outfield positions too soon in life. It might well be that you are not going to be tall enough to be a real goalkeeper later on (not that all keepers *have* to be six-footers!) or you might be a talented athlete who will one day find himself in a team with an even better goalkeeper, but vacancies elsewhere in the side. So practise the other skills, even heading and tackling, until you are 15 or 16 and quite sure that you are a goalkeeper and nothing but a keeper.

Equally those of you who are not goalkeepers would do well to read this chapter, and to take a spell between the posts in practice sometimes; for you never know when you might have to replace an injured keeper. It can be a daunting and lonely experience and if you ever are called upon to substitute you will, I can assure you, have much more respect for your present custodian!

However, the skills involved in keeping goal are of course, quite different from any others. The emphasis is on the hands rather than the feet – though, like me, I suspect that you have seen some remarkable saves with the feet, sometimes with the goalkeeper diving the other way! But a safe pair of hands is the first essential for any young keeper. It is all very well making the spectacular-looking save, but the best goalkeepers are those who *catch* the ball whenever it is possible to do so. In fact, the cardinal principle of goalkeeping is safety first. You should use two hands rather than one whenever you can and you should ensure that your body is behind your hands where possible, as a second line of defence.

There are various ways of catching the ball and no two goalkeepers necessarily use exactly the same technique. Ray Clemence and Peter Shilton for instance both catch the ball in slightly different ways, but both have three things in common whenever possible:

(a) Hands behind the ball (so that a fierce shot or a wet ball does not slip through).

(b) Body behind the ball (so that an unkind bounce or a swerving shot which eludes the hands does not finish in the net).

(c) Eyes on the ball (absolutely vital to any goalkeeper; but easier said than done in a crowded penalty area with forwards challenging and distracting the keeper).

If you neglect these golden rules you will all too frequently allow the ball to squeeze past you into the net – or allow an opponent to follow up and score when you fail to held on to a powerful shot.

The low ground shot is often not quite so easy to save as our goalkeeper in photograph **68** makes it look, but whether you go down on one knee or not, note how the hands and then the legs are behind the ball giving not one, but two lines of defence. Equally it is important to ensure that your body is *behind* the line of the ball when you have to dive to stop a low shot to one side of you. Young schoolboys frequently make the mistake of diving over the top of the ball but if you

68 The double line of defence. Hands *and* legs behind the ball here when collecting the low drive. It looks all too easy but the ball can slither through if the technique is faulty.

69 A good action picture of our young goalkeeper diving to his left to save a low shot. Notice the balance as he prepares to move.

70 Eyes on the ball, hands at the ready, excellent concentration. Sound technique, but perhaps the left shoulder should be nearer the ground. Compare with photograph **72**.

71 The final save, with two lines of defence again – the arms and the body. But I should like to see that ball a little more securely grasped here, in case any opposing forward is following up.

look closely at our young goalkeeper in photographs **69–71** you will see him making a good save to his left. However, if you compare this with our professional in photograph **72** you will see how much more securely he has clutched the ball and how solidly his body is acting as the second line of defence.

A chest or waist high ball, as in photograph **73**, is in a sense easier to deal with, but notice the eyes fixed firmly on the ball, the balanced position of our goalkeeper and again the securely held ball in photograph **74**. Remember that you should try to catch the ball rather

72 Compare this with photographs **70** and **71** and look how firmly the ball is held here.

73 The basic position for a waist high save. Notice how the goalkeeper is welcoming that ball with open arms, eyes concentrating on the job.

74 Only when the ball is firmly grasped should the goalkeeper start to look round and consider his distribution.

than parry it whenever possible, as our schoolboy has done in photograph **75**, though he has slightly mistimed his jump Whereas our professional looks more in control of the shot he is saving in photograph **76**, though to be fair it is not quite such a difficult one to save!

When the shot is above your head, you obviously have to make an instant decision and if there are opposing forwards close at hand, then it might be safer to punch clear or flip the ball over the crossbar for a corner. But again, try to catch the ball when you can. Incidentally do not dive dramatically to save (as some Continental goalkeepers tend to do) if you can reach the ball by taking a couple of quick paces and remain on your feet. It might not look so photogenic, but is far better goalkeeping!

75 Saving a high shot is not always easy. This goalkeeper has quite rightly decided to catch the ball rather than punch it; but the technique would be more convincing if his left arm was above the ball.

76 Saving a high shot made to look easy. Notice how the hands are ready to welcome the ball into the chest – and look at the professional goalkeeper's concentration too.

Naturally you will not always be able to catch the fiercest or cleverest shots, particularly if they are intentionally bent or swerved at you. On such occasions, the safety-first precaution is usually the correct one, to punch clear, or to flip the ball over the bar or round the post. A finger-tip save is one thing and you will know the excitement of flying through the air to save a certain goal, as Ken Mulhearn in photograph **77**. These are instinctive saves, thrilling and often graceful but they cannot be coached.

77 The save that goalkeepers dream about. Plucking the ball out of the air with a full length dive – and holding on to it too!

Correct punching can be coached however. In my experience this is the one technique which schoolboy goalkeepers find most difficult to conquer and the sooner you punch correctly the better. To start with *never* flap at the ball and palm it straight up in the air. For if you do, you might make yourself popular with the opposing forwards, but not with your own defenders. If you are forced to punch the ball clear, when jumping with a tall opponent for instance, or moving out to meet a well-flighted centre, make sure that you keep your eye on the ball (again!), that your arms are straight, not bent and that

[51]

78

79

80

81

82

81–82 *Punching a high centre.* The goalkeeper here has not quite matched the power and authority of the professional in photograph **80**; but this is a good action shot of the one-handed punch clear.

you punch positively as demonstrated so well in photographs **78–82**. Two fists are safer than one, though as you gain in experience you might find, as some of our top goalkeepers do, that you prefer punching with one. If you cannot find the distance to clear your own penalty area, then it would be safer to deflect the ball for a corner. But with practice you will be surprised at the distance you can achieve with a positive punch.

78–80 *Punching a high centre.* In this sequence our professional goalkeeper elects to punch clear under pressure from attackers. Look at the timing of the jump, the eyes and the balance; but note, particularly, the power behind this two-fisted punch.

83

83–85 *Catching a high centre.* In this sequence we can follow the three stages of a perfect catch by our goalkeeper under slightly less pressure than in photograph **79**. You will see the spring, the secure handling, but note, above all, the intense concentration on the ball throughout.

84

85

As with the high shot, so with the lofted centre or corner, if you can catch the ball rather than punch it, then do so. Look at photographs **83–85** and compare them carefully with **78–80**. Only a confident goalkeeper will decide as our professional has done in **84** to catch rather than punch; but look at his technique. Concentration on the ball, the springy leap, the positive handling and above all the complete lack of concern for the other players challenging. Compare this with photograph **86** and note how our school goalkeeper, though jumping high and holding on (just!) might have been better advised to punch here rather than catch. It is always easy to decide these things after the event, but you young goalkeepers must make your decisions in a flash – and stick to them.

86 *Catching a high centre.* Our schoolboy goalkeeper holding onto the ball under pressure. A good save, but might it have been safer to punch clear here? Note incidentally the good cover position of the two full backs.

NARROWING THE ANGLE AND SMOTHERING THE BALL

Knowing when to leave your goal-line and how far to come represent the most crucial aspects of goalkeeping and you will only really learn by experience and match practice. How often have you seen a top class keeper coming way out of his penalty area to clear his lines (or even to tackle) as an opposing forward bursts through? Vice-versa

87 90 *Narrowing the angle and smothering the ball 1.* In this sequence our professional goalkeeper is confronted by an opposing attacker and has to make several rapid decisions.

87 Moving out fast to narrow the angle – but eyes on the ball.

88 Forcing the attacker towards his left – and look at the way our goalkeeper has covered most of his goal.

89 The moment of decision, as the forward hesitates and the ball is within the goalkeeper's reach.

90 Ball firmly grasped; and note how a goalkeeper should try to turn his shoulder as he falls, as a protection against the incoming forward.

91-94 *Narrowing the angle and smothering the ball 2.* Anything the professional can do, so can you, if you keep practising; and here our young goalkeeper emulates Ken Mulhearn.

91 Narrowing the angle, but balanced and pushing the attacker to his right.

92 Preparing to dive, yet ready for any surprise shot. Note that the eyes have never left the ball.

93 As the forward momentarily loses control, our goalkeeper strikes with two hands. A good action shot.

94 The final save, and the ball is safely grasped. However, compare the goalkeeper's position with that of our professional in photograph **90**.

we have all seen the goalkeeper so lacking in confidence that he stays riveted on his own goal-line as a forward bears down on him. However good the defence in front of you, there will be times when an opposing forward is clean through with only the goalkeeper to beat and you will make the attacker's job much more difficult if you 'narrow the angle' and give him the smallest possible target to aim at. One of the vital rules for any keeper in this situation is to make up his mind rapidly whether to come out, or stay on his line (and this applies to centres and corners as well as through passes). But if you come, come quickly, close the forward's target down, but retain your balance – and get your angles right! It is interesting to discover that some professional goalkeepers when racing out to confront an on-coming forward will not go down and dive at their feet at all, but simply stand up as if prepared to tackle the attacker in the manner of an ordinary defender. I am told that it completely perplexes the forward concerned and is sometimes more effective than diving at his feet. Try it – in practice perhaps!

But any good goalkeeper must be brave – no more so than when he is called upon to dive at the feet of a threatening opponent. It is perfectly safe, if you remember to keep your eye on the ball, not to dive in head first, and to tuck your head well in as in photograph **90** once you have clutched the ball to your chest. There are several methods of 'smothering' the attacker in this situation and if you look at photographs **87–94** you will see two splendid sequence shots of our professional and our schoolboy narrowing the angle, forcing the forward to the side they prefer and then committing themselves positively as he tries to dribble round them. You might criticize the young attacker for not shooting earlier but there is much to learn from the balance, concentration and technique of both our goalkeepers in these action shots. Look at them carefully. They are both saving 'certain' goals.

CLEARING THE BALL

As goalkeeper you are the last line of the defence, it is true. But we must not forget that you are also the first line of attack; and the best goalkeepers often set their attack in motion with a long kick to a fast breaking forward, or a quick throw to an unmarked colleague. Obviously, if you have a strong centre forward in your team, a long kick for him to head on (especially with the wind behind you) is thoroughly sensible. But try to acquire the habit of *throwing* a pass when possible – it is a far more constructive way of building an attack, as long as the throw is *quick* and *accurate*. You will need to practise your throwing and it is dangerous to be too ambitious when your arms have not developed their full strength.

In addition too many schoolboy goalkeepers are weak kickers of the dead ball and tend to leave goal-kicks to their full-backs. Do not make the same mistake – a goalkeeper who can kick is a real asset to his team (watch England's Peter Shilton if you are in any doubt). Remember, too, that there are times when you want to use the full extent of your penalty area – when kicking into a strong wind or using a heavy ball – and in this respect it is important to learn to dodge challenging forwards and to use the extra space. Although not all referees necessarily implement the law strictly, you are only allowed four steps with the ball in your hands and you must always be aware of this; and you will frequently be confronted by an opponent trying (fairly, we hope) to prevent you clearing with your strongest foot. All these facets of goalkeeping are too readily neglected and you would be well advised to practise your distribution and your weaving and dodging in the penalty area as much as you do your saving of the ball in the first place.

CALLING

Finally how positively do you call for the ball, or talk to your defenders? A good goalkeeper should be prepared to accept responsibility with such a shout as 'Goalie's ball!' but as he is the one player who can see the whole play developing in front of him, a shout of, 'Watch your winger, Mike!' or 'Your ball, Jim!', will often come as helpful advice to the rest of the defence; and do not forget your part in setting up a defensive wall. But calm, authoritative calling is what you should aim at, not – as many goalkeepers do – frantic and panicky instructions, which only help to encourage your opponents, or produce an own goal! Keeping goal, then, is not just a matter of going out onto the field and making one brilliant save after another, nor is it standing between the posts in practice whilst the rest of your team shoot in. There is much more to it than that, both in preparation and in practice. For instance, do you prepare fully for each particular game? On one of those early autumn days when the sun drops low and shines brightly, have you a cap that fits to help you collect the high ball? On the skiddy, drizzly surfaces of November and December have you the right type of goalkeeper's gloves to help you hold on to the wet ball? Then, when we come to the cold, frosty days of January and February have you remembered to pack two sweaters and some tracksuit trousers? They are all important, if you hope to do your job properly.

Equally it is important that you practise intelligently, working on your own particular weakness and not just playing to your strengths. If you are on the short side you will probably need to concentrate on the high shots and the lofted centres; if you are tall then get your forwards to drive the ball at you low and hard. Remember that goalkeepers quite often are left on their own to practise whilst the rest of the side are concentrating on some outfield skill and it is thus all the more important that you are aware of your weaknesses and know how to work at them.

Practice Routines to Improve your Goalkeeping

(a) There is no better start than returning to our wall (as long as you have somewhere relatively soft to fall). You can sharpen your reactions, check that your hands and body are behind the ball and that you are diving correctly by driving the ball against the wall, at varying heights and saving the rebound. You can also incidently improve your throwing by setting up a target area on the wall and practising overarm throwing, gradually aiming from further and further away.

(b) The next step can be taken by practising in pairs and with one serving and the other saving, you will gain excellent practice in catching, punching, jumping, diving and in quick distribution. But, as I have indicated earlier, these practices will often take place without the coach directing operations and it will be of little value unless you insist upon realistic services from your partner.

(c) In the final reckoning, you want to spend as much of your practising time as possible actually in between the posts in the proper setting of the goal area. Only by hours of practice moving about the goal will you develop that accurate sense of position that is so vital for a keeper. Incidentally, if it can be arranged, it is sometimes not a bad thing to practise in a slightly larger goal than the one you are going to defend in the match itself. As long as it does not wreck your confidence, it can make the ordinary goalmouth seem puny when you come to the big game itself.

There are numerous team practices relating to goalkeepers, too many to list fully here, but do not forget to ask your coach to allow some forwards to dribble at you so that you can try to narrow the angle and perhaps smother the shot; and in my experience the practices dealing with crosses or corners are always invaluable – for defenders and goalkeepers – particularly if the penalty area is gradually filled with players as the practice develops.

Finally do not forget to practise trying to save penalty kicks. They do not (we hope) come very often but when they do, they tend to be crucial and it is amazing how rarely penalty practice is taken seriously.

CHAPTER 7

Applying Skill in the Game

We have looked closely at the technique required and the skill involved in mastering a football; but being able to kick the ball perfectly, to head it correctly and to run with it 'tied to our bootlaces' obviously does not necessarily mean that we are going to be effective footballers in the game itself. This is why I have emphasized the importance of practising in 5-, 6- or 11-a-side game situations as soon as you have learned the techniques themselves. By all means revert to your basic practices from time to time – as a golfer goes back to his professional in order to eliminate a slice or a hook – but never forget that you must be able to apply the skills you have learned, in the middle for the duration of the match.

I cannot, sadly, watch you in your next game and note how much your skill needs improving, or your application of it needs changing; but I will do the next best thing. I can ask you to think selectively and intelligently about how you would react in certain realistic situations on the field of play. I shall ask you to study the simple diagrams below, to look at the questions and decide for yourself what you would do in each instance. There is only one golden rule – the answers are at the end of the chapter and clearly you would gain nothing by looking at them before wrestling with the questions, so do not cheat! You will also note that I have set out the questions in the form of multiple choice and awarded points in the answers accordingly. Finally you (and your coach or your footballing friends) might well disagree with my allocation of points and there are obviously occasions when you might say 'Well! It all depends!', but look closely at the diagrams and sum up the pros and cons and remember that the referee's verdict is final. In any case, if you do argue and discuss the various alternatives, I shall feel satisfied that I have provoked you and others into thinking about applying skill in the game itself and that is what I am aiming at in the following examples.

QUESTION 1

We are on the attack and our right winger O7 has the ball, but is being chased by X3, the opposing full back. If you were O7 should you:

(a) Chip a high centre across the goal towards the far post?

(b) Cut in until you draw a defender and then pull back a low pass to an incoming colleague?

(c) Drive the ball low and hard to the near post?

(d) Slow down, keep possession and wait for support to arrive?

Decide on your order of priorities here and then turn to the answers at the end of this chapter.

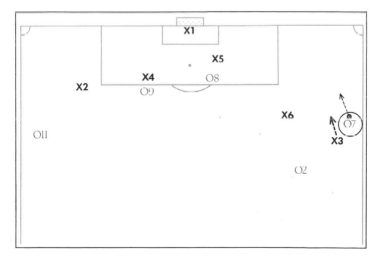

QUESTION 2

Our centre half O5 is standing just inside his own half and is about to receive a long, high punt from the opposing goalkeeper. The centre forward is some 5 metres distant as the ball arrives, but closing in fast. If you were O5 would you:

(a) Volley the ball first time back into the opposing half?
(b) Volley or head the ball to your support centre back O6?
(c) Head the ball back into the opposing half?
(d) Trap the ball and if so with the head, foot, thigh or chest?

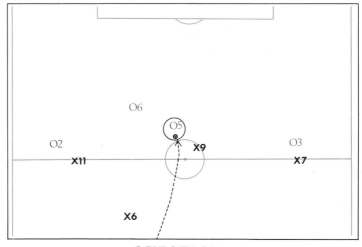

QUESTION 3

Here is a question for goalkeepers. We have a corner against us taken by X7 on the right. You are O1 and you have the normal defensive cover around you, but have to contend with a typically crowded penalty area. The dotted line marks the course of the lofted away swing corner. If you were O1 would you:

(a) Come out and catch the ball?
(b) Come out and punch it?
(c) Come halfway but leave it to your defenders when you realize that it is curving away from you?
(d) Stay on your goal-line and leave it to your defenders to head clear?

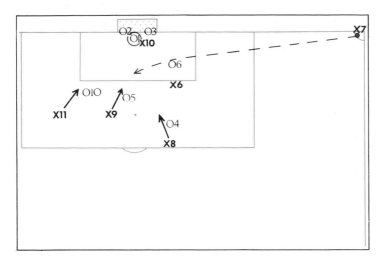

QUESTION 4

Our full back O2 has the opposing winger coming at him with the ball. He is a good dribbler with a strong left foot and has already beaten O4. Our cover defence is not yet organized as we have been attacking and our opponents have broken away quickly. If you were O2 would you:

(a) Tackle straight away?
(b) Force X11 down the touchline and tackle if or when the chance arises?
(c) Force X11 across field and tackle if or when the chance arises?
(d) Back off and jockey him until you reach the edge of your penalty area and then tackle?

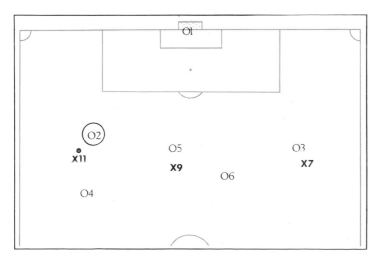

QUESTION 5

Our centre forward O9 has just received a low pass from defence, and as we can see from the diagram he is quite tightly marked by X5. If you were O9 would you:

(a) Pass back (lay off) first time to O8 or O6?
(b) Pass back to O8 or O6 after you have controlled the ball?
(c) Turn and attempt to take on your opposing centre half?
(d) Dribble sideways or backwards away from X5?
(e) Shield and screen the ball until a decisive pass appears?

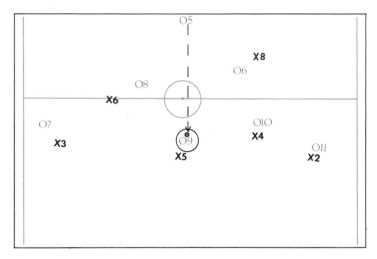

QUESTION 6

Our defender O6 has the ball facing his own goal and is being challenged by the opposing forward X8. We are winning 1-0 with 5 minutes or so remaining. If you were O6 would you:

(a) Pass back to the goalkeeper?
(b) Pass back to our left back O3?
(c) Half turn and pass to O8?
(d) Turn and dribble your way out of trouble?
(e) Put the ball out of play and over the stand if possible?

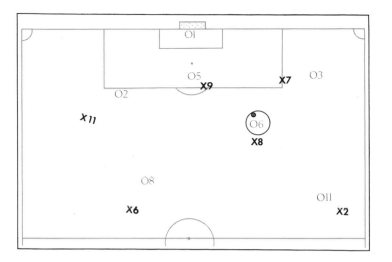

QUESTION 7

We have the ball in midfield with O8. His marker X6 has pushed too far upfield and O8 finds some space (about 10–15 metres) in front of him. If you were O8 would you:

   (a) Slow the game down and wait for one of your forwards to make a decisive run before passing?

   (b) Play a long through ball behind X2 to our left winger O11?

   (c) Play an early pass to the feet of O7 or O9 and run for the return?

   (d) Dribble fast at the opposing defence, only passing when you draw a defender to you?

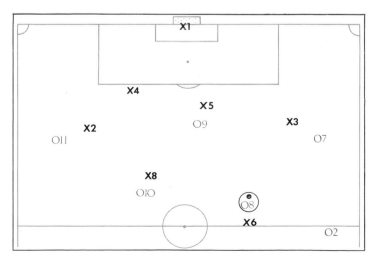

QUESTION 8

We have just won possession of the ball and our full back O3 is coming forward with it at his feet. X7 is in attendance – O11, O4 and O1 are all available for a pass, while O9 is already making a run out to the left touchline. If you were O3 would you:

    (a) Look for O9 with a lofted ball into the space behind X2?
    (b) Play a short, firm ball to the feet of our winger O11?
    (c) Turn the ball square to O4 or back to goalkeeper O1?
    (d) Take on X7 and attempt to dribble past him?

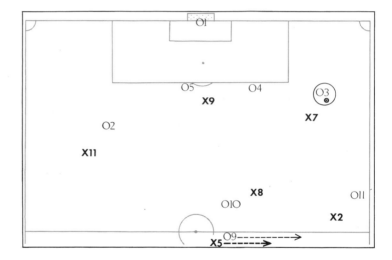

QUESTION 9

We have been attacking down the right side of the field and our winger O7 has the ball near the touchline closely guarded by the opposing full back X3. As you can see from the diagram there are several of our players free. If you were O7 would you:

    (a) Stab a side footed ball to O9 or O10, run on and look for a return pass?
    (b) Turn and play the ball back to O2?
    (c) Hit a direct long pass out to our left winger O11?
    (d) Give a short pass to O8 so that he can switch the play to O11?

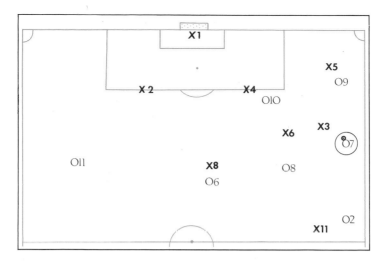

QUESTION 10

We have a direct free kick just outside the penalty area. The opposition have set up a 'wall' with four defenders in it and the tall men on both sides (O9, O5, X6 and X9) are waiting for a possible header in the penalty area. O4 steps up to take the kick with O10 in attendance. You probably all have a favourite free kick in your team, and there is nothing more satisfying than seeing the kick you have worked at in practice achieve a goal in the match itself. But in this situation if you were O4 which type of kick would you use?

(a) The angled chip for O9 and O5 to run onto and head at goal?
(b) The low driven ball for O7 to run onto behind defender X8?
(c) The bent or curved shot around the right edge of the wall?
(d) The side footed pass for O10 (or O8) to make use of?

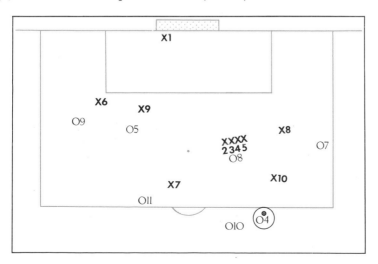

QUESTION 11

Our left winger O11 has the ball and has stolen a yard or two on his opposing full back. There are several of our forwards in the centre waiting for a cross. If you were O11 would you:

(a) Centre as soon as possible with a low driven ball for O10 to run onto?

(b) Centre as soon as possible with a chip for O9 to meet with his head?

(c) Centre as soon as possible with a long lofted pass aimed at O7?

(d) Delay your centre until more of our forwards are closer to goal?

(e) Make for the bye-line and then pull back a ground pass for O6 to run onto?

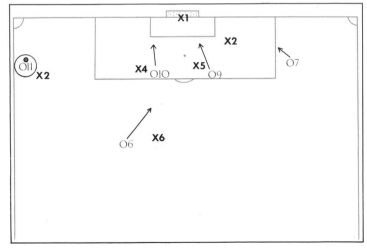

QUESTION 12

We have possession of the ball in the centre circle with O8 in control. There seem to be plenty of options open here because our opponents are not marking as tightly as they should and we have plenty of colleagues screaming for a pass. If you were O8 would you:

(a) Pass to O10's feet?

(b) Pass to O7's feet?

(c) Pass to O9's feet?

(d) Play a through ball in front of O4?

(e) Play a through ball in front of O3?

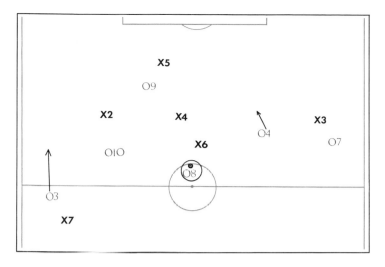

QUESTION 13

Our winger here O7 has got round his full back and reached the bye-line (where all you young wingers ought to be aiming!). His driven cross (arrowed above) reaches O9 at waist height as he moves forward. If you were O9 would you:

(a) Try to volley the ball at goal?
(b) Attempt a header at goal, diving if necessary?
(c) Control the ball quickly and aim to shoot?
(d) Flick the ball on for O10 or knock it back for O8 to shoot?

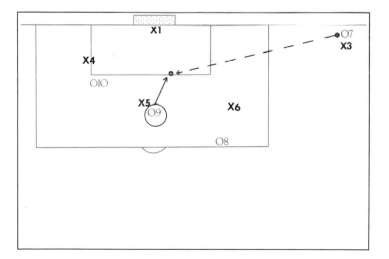

QUESTION 14

We do not need a diagram in this question and once again it is aimed primarily at the goalkeeper. We are 2-1 down with only about five minutes of the match remaining. Our keeper has just saved the ball and if you were in his position would you:

    (a) Get rid of the ball as quickly as possible in the general direction of our opponent's goal?

    (b) Use your area and then kick long and high downfield?

    (c) Throw the ball to an unmarked colleague as quickly as you can?

    (d) Dribble upfield yourself?

QUESTION 15

One of our strikers, in this case O11, has been given a chance to run at the opposing goal. As you can see in the diagram only X6, whose strong foot is his left, stands between O11 and a shot on goal. Support is arriving but there is no positive pass available yet. If you were O11 would you:

    (a) Wait for the support to arrive and then pass to O9, O7 or O10?

    (b) Run at X6 fast and aim to sprint past him?

    (c) Run at X6 then accelerate past him on the left side?

    (d) Run at X6 then change speed and go past him on the right side as you look at him?

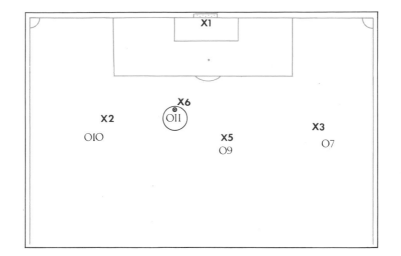

QUESTION 16

We are up against a clever forward line and our midfield player O6 has had a problem marking the elusive ball player X8. As the ball is being played to X8 by one of his defenders and he moves towards it (as any good player always should) if you were O6 would you:

    (a) Stay where you are and wait for him to turn and come at you?
    (b) Go with him and try to intercept the ball before it reaches him?
    (c) Go with him and keep goal-side of him, but tight enough to stop him turning when he takes possession?

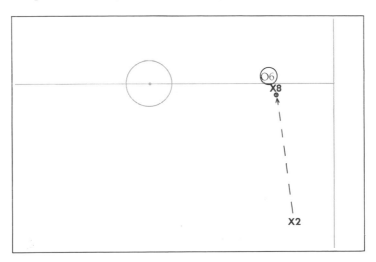

QUESTION 17

In this example one of our strikers, O9 has reached the bye line and is cutting in towards goal. Support has arrived and as you will see in the diagram the penalty area is becoming crowded. If you were O9 would you:

(a) Pull the ball back along the ground to O8?
(b) Chip the ball into the middle for O6, O11 or O10 to head?
(c) Drive the ball low and hard across the face of the goal?
(d) Shoot?

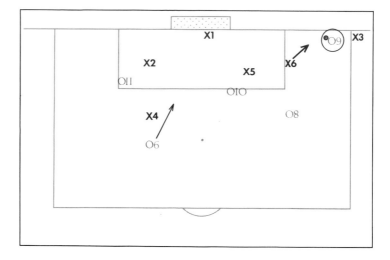

QUESTION 18

A slightly different sort of question here, concerned with skill 'off the ball', the skill of positioning yourself correctly. In the diagram we can see our opponents building up an attack down their left wing and X11 has the ball. O6 is our cover centre half. Where should he be positioning himself?

(a) Position O6a?
(b) Position O6b?
(c) Position O6c?
(d) Position O6d?

[74]

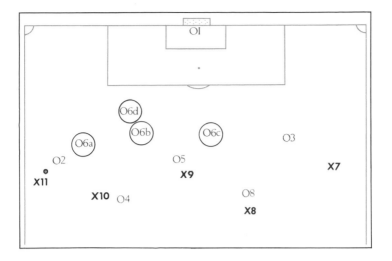

QUESTION 19

Again we are looking here at movement 'off the ball'. This time let us consider our centre forward O9, waiting to receive a pass as our midfield players build up the attack, but finding himself tightly marked by the opposing centre half X5. In the diagram situation, what would you do if you were centre forward and O10 has the ball:

  (a) Move to position O9a?
  (b) Move to position O9b?
  (c) Move to position O9c?
  (d) Move to position O9d?
  (e) Stay where you are?

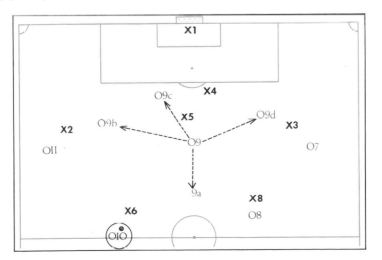

QUESTION 20

Finally a positional question for the goalkeeper. The opposing centre forward X9 is clear through and is advancing fast from just outside the penalty area pursued by O5. If you were our goalkeeper O1 would you:

   (a) Move fast towards X9?

   (b) Move slowly towards him?

   (c) Move as fast as you can, but steady yourself 2 metres or so from him?

   (d) Move fast until 5 metres from him then advance cautiously?

   (e) Stay on your line and pray?

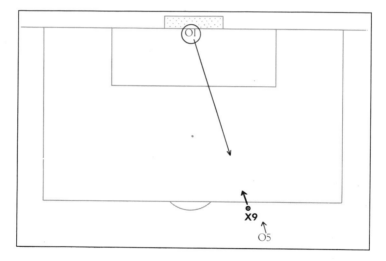

ANSWER 1

There are not sufficient forwards in the opposing penalty box for a high chipped centre and the attack would lose its momentum if O7 slowed down by the touchline and waited for support. The low driven cross is often a rewarding one, but O8 and O9 would have to cover a lot of ground to make use of such a pass in this diagram. (b) is the best plan of attack here, as our winger O7 has a clear run in towards goal. If he moves fast, keeps ahead of full back X3, he will draw out one of the opposing defenders X4, X5 or X6 and should find O8, O9 or even O2 in support for a diagonal pulled back pass from the goal-line and with a clear shot on goal.

Thus (b) 5 points
(c) 2
(a) 1
(d) 0

ANSWER 2

The goalkeeper's kick is bound to produce a dropping ball and this might prove very difficult to volley cleanly upfield. Equally it would be even more dangerous for O5 to risk a first time pass to O6 or to any of his defenders for that matter; any slight misjudgement here and X9 would be through on his own and O5 would be left holding his head in his hands. A highly skilled centre back might consider trapping the ball, but receiving a kick from some distance, he would be crazy to cushion it on his head, foolhardy to try the thigh or chest trap and if he did bring it under control with his foot he would need to 'kill' it dead, before X9 pounced. (c) is the safest decision here as O5 has probably more chance of directing a header than a volley to one of our forwards.

Thus (c) 5
(d) 3 (for a trap with the feet)
1 (with the chest)
(a) 1
(b) 0

ANSWER 3

The arc of the kick, the wind, the height of the opposing forwards, your own confidence with high balls and any split second developments make it impossible to be absolute about this one. But no real goalkeeper should fall between two stools and leave himself stranded halfway. This is poor goalkeeping – either come the whole way or stay. Even though the ball is curving away from the goal, a positive keeper ought to take responsibility for any cross in his six-yard area and it would be an over-cautious one who stays put on his goal-line. Whether to punch or catch? A good firm punch might well be the answer particularly if you find your centre back and the centre forward jumping high; but always catch if possible and therefore I suggest that (a) is the best answer in this situation.

Thus (a) 5
     (b) 3
     (d) 1
     (c) 0

ANSWER 4

As we have seen from the diagram there is no cover yet available, although O4 (when he has picked himself up) and O6 should be recovering as fast as they possibly can; so it would be dangerous to risk a tackle straightaway, especially if X11 has good close control. Also we have already discovered that he possesses a strong left foot and he will therefore almost certainly want to beat O2 on the outside, so do not let him. We must delay him then, and the safest way to do this is to jockey him and back off hoping that cover reappears before he reaches the edge of our penalty area. However, if the winger X11 has a weak right foot, it might well be the best policy to force him across field, thus slowing him up and then to tackle decisively when he loses control on the weaker right foot. So, although (d) is a sound answer here, the intelligent full back will probably opt for (c).

[78]

Thus (c) 5
     (d) 4
     (b) 1
     (a) 0

ANSWER 5

Any positive centre forward should try to turn and go at his centre half whenever possible – never forget this! But in this situation we have noticed how tightly X_5 is shadowing O_9 and even allowing for our centre forward moving towards the ball as he receives it, he is hardly going to be able to turn successfully here. Nor does it help our attack much if O_9 starts to dribble backwards (or even sideways). This will slow the momentum of attack and is exactly what X_5 is hoping to see O_9 do! Screening the ball is an important art for any centre forward and is vital when he receives the ball and is waiting for support to arrive; but, in this instance, support has arrived already and we can see from the diagram that both O_8 and O_6 are temporarily free for a quick return pass. It would have to be quick however and first time if possible, because X_6 and X_8 will soon be marking their opposite numbers if O_9 waits to control the ball first. So (a) is certainly the best decision here, especially if the lay off is followed by a positive run by O_9.

Thus (a) 5
     (c) 2
     (e) 2
     (b) 1
     (d) 0

ANSWER 6

Too many teams one goal ahead with little time remaining would be thinking only of defending and 'holding on to the points'. They would be tempted to bang the ball out of play and perhaps waste a moment or two. But this is negative thinking and will often, in the end, encourage your opponents to get back in the game. On the other hand to try to turn and dribble your way out of trouble in this situation is very over ambitious. X8 might rob you and go through for the equalizer. Trying to find O8 is understandable but requires tight control and good skill; whereas playing the ball back to the goalkeeper here, even with a chip is a little risky given the positions of opposing forwards X9 and X7 in the diagram. No, answer (b) is much the best answer here – a safe, constructive and controlled pass in the path of our left back O3.

> Thus (b)   5
>   (c)   2
>   (a)   1
>   (e)   0
>   (d) −1

ANSWER 7

Once you have lost your marker (in this case X6) it would be foolish to slow the game down because you will allow him to recover and possibly tackle you while you delay. A quick pass is often a good plan for any player – although it always requires sound technique – and you might find that a firm ball to O9 or O7 leads to a shot on goal, but such a pass would make more sense if O8 was more closely challenged. As it is, the long through ball to O11 could split the opposing defence and allow our winger to reach the bye-line. This would be a good pass to look for, but over 30 metres or so with other players likely to intercept, it would have to be chipped perfectly into the gap behind the opposing right back X2. However, if you find space in front of you, as is the case here, it is usually right to make the most of it and I suggest that (d) is the best option in this situation and that O8 should dribble fast at the defence drawing an opponent (probably X5) and *then* slipping a more telling pass to O9.

> Thus (d)   5
>   (b)   2
>   (c)   1
>   (a)   0

ANSWER 8

I have encouraged you earlier on to use your dribbling skills, but your own half is not the best place to gamble, particularly if you are likely to leave the opposing winger X7 with a free run on goal if you fail. No, do not dribble here! Equally there are times when a back pass to your goalkeeper or a square pass might make sense, *but only when nothing is available going forward.* In any case, no full back should ever play a square ball across his own back four; a back or angled pass is safer. The low pass to O11 is safe enough, particularly if O3 then moves quickly in support; but the most positive answer here is (a) the chipped pass into space down the left touchline, especially if your centre forward is aware of the value of running wide occasionally.

Thus (a)   5
     (b)   2
     (c)   1
     (d) — 1

ANSWER 9

You have only to look at the diagram to realize that space is very cramped on one side of the field and wide open on the other – a point we often neglect when we are actually playing. Clearly a 'push and run' pass with O9 or O10 might lead to a shot on goal and is worth considering, but both of them are well marked here. A pass back to O2 retains possession for us, but does not help us to switch play into the open spaces. No, it would be ideal to give an *immediate* long ball to our left winger O11, but you would have to deliver the crossfield pass as powerfully and accurately as Bobby Charlton if you hoped to play it direct from one side of the field to the other. The best way to exploit the spaces around O11, is probably to find O8 with an angled pass (behind him to avoid the likely challenge from marker X6); O8 could then control, screen it, turn and hit a lofted 30-metre pass to O11. So the best answer here is (d) and the quicker we switch the play the more problems our left winger can set the opposing defence.

Thus (d)   5
     (a)   3
     (c)   2
     (b)   1

ANSWER 10

It is never a bad rule when taking a free kick to keep things as simple as possible. The low driven ball for our winger O7 to run onto does not leave much margin for error, and then is unlikely to lead to a direct shot on goal. The properly flighted chip to O9 and O5 could produce a headed goal, and is well worth considering, but remember that the opposition have their big men waiting for this. Equally the side footed pass, though more accurate, is unlikely to give O8 a direct shot on goal and O10, while having a clear sight of the target, will have to strike the ball on the move perfectly. Not an easy shot, but often the best option. In this case however, although the lob over the wall is only worth a try if the opposing goalkeeper is known to be slow, look at the wall more closely and you will see that the end man is lined up directly between the ball and the goalpost. This is incorrect, for it leaves room for the slightly bent shot on goal and if you have been practising your curved kicking then (c) is the best option here.

Thus (c)   5
     (e)   3 (for O10)
           2 (for O8)
     (a)   2
     (b)   1
     (d)   1

ANSWER 11

This is not an easy one because our decision must depend upon the timing of O9 and O10's running. What it does emphasize however is the importance of 'running off the ball' which we were considering in the last chapter. It also highlights the vital need for O11 to look up before he makes his decision. How often we see wingers cleverly beating their full back, but then running head down, unaware of an unmarked colleague in the penalty area! Equally it is a mistake to delay a centre too long. Your central strikers will want the cross in front of them to run onto and it will only help the opposing defence if you wait for the six-yard area to fill up. A low driven ball for O10 to flick on, or volley at goal is always worth looking for and should certainly be used as a variation to the high centre, but the angle is not quite right for it here. The pull back from the bye-line is another commendable variation, catching defenders on the wrong foot; but there are more immediate strikes at goal available in this diagram. If you chip the ball perfectly to coincide with your centre forward O9's run at goal then he might well be able to head for goal (downwards from the hips remember). But in this situation, as O7 is completely unmarked I would be tempted to float over the long cross to our outside right and he can then either cut in and shoot, or better still, perhaps, head the ball square for O9 or O10 to shoot home.

Thus (c)   5
    (b)   3
    (a)   3
    (e)   2
    (d)   0

ANSWER 12

You will not often be faced with a defence as loose as this, so make the most of it! But we are frequently tempted in this sort of situation to play the safe ball to feet – perhaps because we have seen the professionals do it all too often. Indeed passes to O7, O10 or O9 (who might even turn and attack his opposing centre half X5) are all perfectly respectable ones – we still have possession. But never forget that, however many players are shouting for the ball, *if* you spot a telling through pass *always* take the direct route for goal if it is there. So, in this instance an angled through ball to our left back O3 would leave him free to reach the bye-line and to cause havoc from there. But even more decisive would be a chipped through ball in the path of O4 – who has incidentally, like O3, made a fine run off the ball –

and although it would require vision, courage and skill (d) would be the best choice here.

Thus (d)   5
     (e)   3
     (c)   3
     (a)   1
     (b)   1

ANSWER 13

It is not always easy to decide how to deal with a ball coming at such an awkward height, but one thing is certain that if you choose in this situation to pass the responsibility of shooting to O10 or O8, then you should never be a centre forward! You must always shoot when half a chance arises and this is more like a full chance. It would be safer to control the ball first and smack it into goal, but X5 is not far away. Lack of time and space dictate that you should shoot first time. If you have decided upon the waist-high volley, good luck to you! It is a very difficult skill indeed and although you might break the back of the net you are more likely to hit the roof of the grand stand unless your knee is over the ball as you strike it. On the edge of the six-yard box you are close enough to punch a low header at goal, and if you can stoop rather than dive all the better. So (b) is the best option here.

Thus (b)   5
     (a)   3
     (c)   1
     (d)   0

ANSWER 14

If you chose to take on the opposition yourself, it certainly shows courage and imagination and it would be fun to watch, but not perhaps very sensible. In such situations with time running out the immediate reaction of spectators and often players alike is to shout to the keeper to kick the ball as quickly and as far as he can towards the opponent's goal, but this all too often simply gives the ball away and we have achieved nothing. It makes more sense to use the full extent of your penalty area and aim for our centre forward's head, particularly if he is strong in the air. But even with such little time remaining, the most sensible decision is probably (c) and to ensure possession by building up an attack from the back.

Thus (c) 5
    (b) 3
    (a) 1
    (d) 1 (for enterprise)

ANSWER 15

Obviously your decision here will depend to some extent on your own speed and the tactics of X6. If he keeps on backing away, why bother to go past him at all? Keep going at him, just wait until he backs too far into the penalty area and shoot past the (by then) un-sighted keeper. But this is not one of our options here because X6 is too canny. He hopes to delay you until other defenders are back and covering, so he would be particularly happy if you decided to slow it down and wait for support to arrive. No, you must attack him, but how? If you run at him too fast from a distance, he will more easily be able to read your intentions and you will not be able to change pace effectively as you round him. So which of the other options looks most likely? Cutting past him on the right side has the attraction of being the shortest route to goal and might produce the shot you are looking for; but as you have discovered that he is much stronger on his left foot than his right and you as an outside left are probably stronger on your left anyway, why not drag him towards the right side and then accelerate past him on the left? I suggest that (c) is the best plan here – and it is always worth studying your imme-diate opponent's strengths and weaknesses early in the game.

Thus (c) 5
    (d) 3
    (b) 2
    (a) 0

ANSWER 16

This is a very important one, because it raises the whole question of good and bad marking. The feeblest decision here is to stay put, let X8 turn and run at you. You should only leave the player you are marking *if* you are certain that you have handed him over to one of your colleagues. Should you try to reach the ball first? Ask any forward what he prefers, the defender who wants to win the ball or the one who is content just to mark tight. Obviously O6 must not rush in recklessly and if X8 is moving fast to meet the pass, then there might never be any hope of our intercepting it. But *always* try to get to the ball before the forward you are marking, and if you happen to take ball and opponent at the same time – not to worry (as long as it is fair!). Your skilful opponent will soon feel less confident if you mark and tackle positively.

Thus (c) 5
(b) 3
(a) 0

ANSWER 17

There are always temptations to shoot in this sort of position and occasionally poor goalkeeping allows the ball to slip in by the near post, but it is a rather selfish choice and rarely pays dividends. In this case the chip is hardly worth considering because space is so cramped and O9 is already on the edge of the penalty area himself. Which of the other alternatives have you decided upon, the pull back or the low drive? They are both real possibilities and always likely to prove dangerous. If it were wet and slippery I should be inclined to favour the square driven cross for even if our forwards fail to make contact, there is an excellent chance of an own goal. The pull back to O8 is never easy for defenders to adjust to and will be particularly effective if O9 draws X6 while O8 checks his forward run to give himself a little extra space. My vote therefore goes marginally to plan (a).

Thus (a) 5
    (c) 4
    (b) 1
    (d) 0

ANSWER 18

The defensive system you use in your team will naturally influence your decision here. Some teams play a sweeper, others man to man marking and some simply rely upon cover from the full backs. But in this instance we must note three things. Firstly O3 our left back is beginning to cover round behind O5, secondly X10 is threatening to burst through without being properly marked by O4, and thirdly X11 with the ball can see plenty of space behind our full back O2. So O6 must take up a position somewhere in that gap so that he can cover both O2 and O5 and keep an eye on X10. If he moves into O6a he will cover O2 well, but leaves O5 rather vulnerable in the centre; whereas if he takes up the position O6d he will be lying too deep to be of any immediate assistance. So I suggest that O6b is the best cover position here, for you still have time to move across and tackle X11 if he goes past our full back.

Thus (b) 5
    (d) 3
    (a) 2
    (c) 0

ANSWER 19

The important thing to remember here is that when you make a run in football you must not necessarily expect a pass. You will often open up a gap for one of your team mates to exploit. The vital factor is to move somewhere and *never* just to stand still. Even running into the position which O9d has taken up might leave a central space for one of our other forwards to run into; although O10 would find it difficult to reach you there. Do not be frightened of back-tracking towards your own goal as O9a has done, but if you can go forward do. What about the run made by O9c then? Positive enough, but probably covered more easily by X5 and there is also a possibility that you will run offside here. O9b is often the best run in this situation, leaving a space in the centre again and linking up with O11 perhaps. But it does depend upon O10 timing and weighting his pass carefully to coincide with O9's run.

Thus (b)   5
      (c)   3
      (a)   2
      (d)   1
      (e)   —1

ANSWER 20

You might well pray in this situation, but *not* while you are still dithering on your goal-line. Of course, any self-respecting goalkeeper must narrow the angle as quickly as possible – and this is why a goalie should read the game outside his penalty area as well as in, so that he can move out decisively when necessary. Moving out slowly to narrow the angle is better than not moving at all, but it still gives the opposing centre forward X9 plenty of time to pick his spot. Equally he will be happy enough to find a goalkeeper rushing at him from too far away. A neat side-step and an empty net awaits him. No, O1 should move fast but then steady himself, waiting for X9 to panic, lose control or try a shot. But at 2 metres or 5 metres? It is impossible to be exact here, but you would leave more of the goal visible to X9 if you stopped 5 metres away, and you always want to get as close as possible so that you can pounce if the centre forward loses control. So (c) is the best advice here – and remember that if you do slow X9 in his advance, your centre half O5 might well catch and tackle him, and your job will be done without dirtying your knees!

Thus (c)   5
      (d)   3
      (a)   2
      (b)   1
      (e)   —2

CHAPTER 8

Learning from the Coach

It is a mistake to concern yourself too much with tactics and systems when you are young, but as you improve your skill and as you watch the experts more closely, you will realize that the best footballers are those who possess both skill *and* tactical awareness. Perhaps you have already had a tactics talk from your coach, or from the master in charge of your school team; perhaps your side already play 4-3-3, 4-2-4 or 4-4-2; possibly you play the sweeper system or man to man rather than 'zonal' marking. Whatever your position on the field and however successful your team formation, you will make a more complete player if you understand basic tactics and if you listen to your coach. But never forget that *tactics and formations should be moulded around individual players – NOT vice-versa.*

The best coaches are flexible in their use of tactics and will never limit a player's skill and imagination in order to fit into a system. Brian Clough and Peter Taylor are a fine example of this. There were no oppressive and stifling tactics in Nottingham Forest's approach during their years of triumph in 1978–79. Certainly they were well organized in defence, used several well coached set pieces and played a fluid 4-3-3 formation; but, above all, they were encouraged to play to each other's strengths. There was a good balance in the side and an underlying confidence. Yet whether we are talking of such managers as Alf Ramsey, Jock Stein, Bob Paisley, Bobby Robson or Brian Clough we find that they have one thing in common – man management. No team is going to give of its best unless the coach has motivated the players. The great coach will inspire the right sort of team spirit, appoint a respected captain and bring his side to the peak of condition for the crucial game. He will know how to handle individual problems, when to criticize and when to praise and he will have the courage to discipline one of his own players when necessary. He will also have to decide which (if any) of the following systems his team should adopt:

TEAM FORMATIONS
(1) *The 4-2-4 formation*
Ever since it was introduced by Brazil in the 1958 World Cup, 4-2-4 has been a most popular team system, and certainly provides a strong defensive barrier. As figure 1 makes clear, it consists of a defensive unit of four (full backs and two centre backs); two 'link' men in midfield (normally an inside forward and a wing half) and four thrusting forwards. It is a particularly good method of countering a double centre forward menace from your opponents and, if working pro-

Figure 1

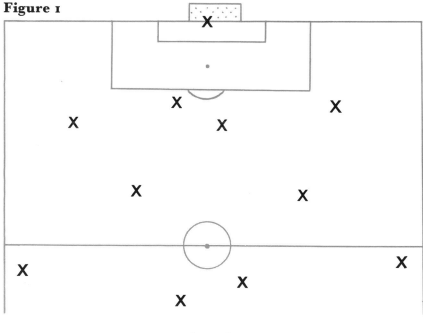

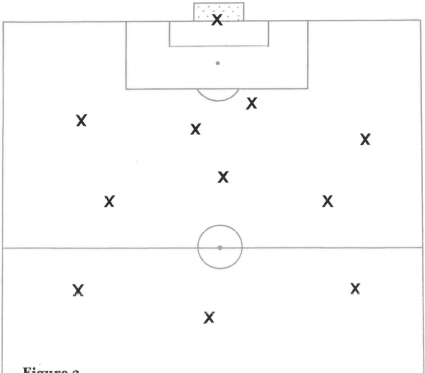

Figure 2

perly, it should give you six players in attack and six in defence when needed. But, this system throws an enormous amount of work upon the two 'link' men and unless they possess great stamina and outstanding ball control, the 4–2–4 formation can backfire very sadly.

(2) *The 4–3–3 formation*

The 4–3–3 system sprang into prominence with England's victory in the 1966 World Cup and immediately many teams adopted Sir Alf Ramsey's formation without realizing the advantages and disadvantages of the system. Defensively the rearguard of four is exactly similar to the defensive line of 4–2–4; but, as you can see, in 4–3–3 another thrusting forward is pulled back to give your team three players linking in mid-field (see figure 2). This means that seven

[91]

players (the rear four and the midfield three) are available for defence and six (the front three and midfield three) for attack if necessary. But, again, it is all to easy to allow this to become a strong defensive system, while the attack is outnumbered.

In 4–3–3 (and many of the variations on this) it is essential for one or more of the midfield three, or one of the full backs, to strike from behind in order to penetrate a close marking defence and this is why we hear so much about overlapping and why we nowadays find so many defenders making and scoring goals in their opponent's penalty area. But remember that in a well-organized team, no defender moves up into attack unless a colleague drops back to cover him.

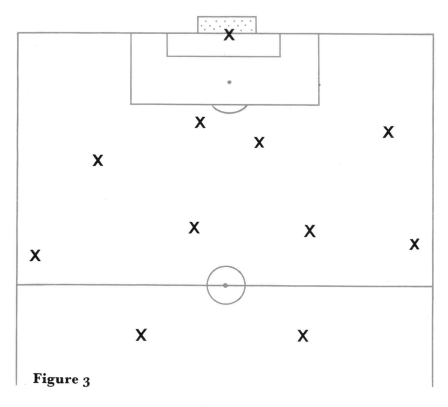

Figure 3

(3) The 4-4-2 formation

In recent years many teams have switched from 4-2-4 and 4-3-3 to 4-4-2 and although this looks a very defensive formation on paper, under an adventurous coach with the right players it can provide attractive, attacking football. Once again our defensive four operate as they should in any other system; but the great strength of 4-4-2 lies in its midfield control. Liverpool have used this system with particular effect, especially when playing away from home in European Cup competitions and, as any coach will tell you, a side that controls midfield is halfway to winning the game. Yet 4-4-2 depends upon the quality of the two front players. They must be highly mobile, prepared to move across the pitch, rather than towards their own goal and strong enough to hold and screen the ball until support arrives. Like 4-3-3, it is absolutely crucial in 4-4-2 to use the touch-lines and stretch the opposing defence and it is no good your team using this formation unless your midfield players come forward and score goals. Above all, your right and left midfield players (see figure 3) or your full backs must keep attacking down the wings.

In defence your coach should encourage you either to mark your opponents 'man for man' or to adopt the 'zonal' system. In the first place you simply follow your immediate opponent all over the field if necessary; whereas in the second, you stay in your 'zone' of the field and mark whichever opposing player enters it. Many European teams, such as the Germans and the Italians, prefer the 'man for man' marking system, but if your team are playing it, remember that forwards must chase back and mark closely as well. British clubs on the whole prefer the 'zonal' system, but this depends upon handing over opposing players as they move out of your zone into that of your fellow defender.

Another very common position in football today is that of sweeper. The 'sweeper' is simply a deep-lying defender who 'sweeps up' behind his defensive line, not marking any particular opponent, but covering his full backs or his central defence. A sweeper can be employed in a 4-2-4, 4-3-3 or 4-4-2 formation, with the centre half marking tight and the other sweeping, but he is increasingly used in

[93]

an even more defensive system, shown in figure 4, sweeping up behind
a line of four other defenders, usually known as the Catenaccio
system. Thus we find many modern teams – especially when playing
away from home – adopting a heavily defensive formation of 1–4–3–2,
which sometimes becomes one sweeper – eight defenders – one
attacker! What a bore for the spectators!

You cannot blame professional clubs (whose livelihood the game
is) for becoming so defensively cautious; but, whatever formation
your team adopts, remember that football is at its best when it is
played as an attacking game – as the Brazilians of 1958, the Dutch
of 1974 and 1978 and the Argentinians in 1978 so wonderfully
reminded us.

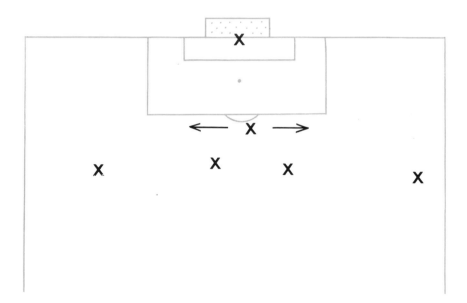

Figure 4

CHAPTER 9

Learning from the Professionals

(1) *Preparing for a match*

The professional footballer walks onto the centre of the stage on the match day and as we watch him with 30,000 other spectators we often envy the excitement and glamour of his life. But the big match occurs usually only once or twice a week and you would do well to remember the hours of training, hard work and careful preparation that go on behind the scenes. In fact just as you should watch and learn from the experts on the pitch itself, so you ought to listen and learn from them in their preparation for a game. Naturally you should not – as a schoolboy – put football first and everything else second, but there are ways in which you can improve your performance by preparing yourself fully for the match day.

FITNESS

Firstly fitness. Some of us are naturally blessed with more stamina than others; but we can all improve our fitness so that we are able to contribute as much in the last five minutes of a hard game as in the first five. What do we learn from the professional's approach to fitness training? I suggest that the following five points are particularly worth noting:

(a) You will not improve your fitness in one exhausting session; it should be a continual process.

(b) The type of training you attempt should be relevant to the 'stop-go' of football and not simply a preparation for cross-country running. It is never a bad thing to start the season with a 2- or 3-mile run; but short, sharp sprints interspersed with jogging or walking are far more valuable. Indeed if you are getting fit on your own, there is still no substitute for these 'winders' – sprint 15 metres and then jog, very slowly, 15 metres – repeating the process until you are exhausted. After all, when you think about it, this is what football is all about, stopping and starting.

(c) The next point to remember when learning from professional training routines, is that they strengthen the muscles, joints and tendons, which are particularly used in kicking and heading. So should you. This means spending time going through these exercises *before* you start sprinting or practising with a ball. Your coach, or your P.E. Master at school, will always show you these helpful exercises – there are many different variations – but they are essential in preparing your body for the match day. If you have especially weak thigh, stomach or neck muscles then it might be worth asking your coach whether he could give you some regular exercises to strengthen them. Possibly a weight circuit, although you should never use weights without first taking expert advice. The professionals spend a lot of time training in this manner.

(d) We all prefer training with a ball rather than without, and it is often possible to combine fitness routines with ball practice. But there is a danger of practising too much and of training too hard. Professional footballers lose their sharpness and their enthusiasm for the game, just as you will, if you spend too much time training beforehand. Your coach might not always agree with me here, but I suggest that you should never expend much energy on the day before a match; and it should go without saying, that an early night (for the professionals too!) and a light (or early) lunch before the match is essential. It is no good training hard during the week, then staying up half Friday night and tucking in to a vast meal half an hour before the Saturday afternoon kick-off!

(e) A word or two about injuries. The treatment of footballing injuries and the speed of recovery have become crucial factors in the modern professional game; and naturally we are all as keen as mustard to be back playing our favourite game as soon as we possibly can. If you are unfortunate enough to break a leg, or need stitches in your forehead, time must obviously dictate your recovery. But, as a general rule, if you pull or strain a muscle or twist an ankle, the quicker you have it treated the better and an immediate ice compress will often help to reduce any swelling and perhaps knock two or three days off your recovery time. However, three warnings: do not make a fuss about nothing; do not risk using the sort of anaesthetic sprays which the professional uses unless you have special permission to do so; and do not forget to see your doctor or a physiotherapist if the injury is a persistent one.

When the professionals have finished their fitness training and skills practice during the week, a great deal of time and trouble goes into the care and preparation of their boots and their kit. It makes an enormous difference if a team looks the part as it appears at the start of a match; whether we are talking about an international eleven appearing from the tunnel in front of 100,000 spectators, or you and your school team emerging from your changing rooms to play against your local rivals in front of a handful of faithful fans. Do you check these points before you trot out onto the pitch:

(a) That you have clean kit?

(b) That your boots have the right studs for the occasion? Moulded rubber studs are no help at all if the pitch is heavy and wet, just as long studs will only give you blisters if the ground is bone hard.

(c) Have you tied your boots properly with the knot or bow well away from the kicking area on your foot? It is remarkable how many young footballers neglect this vital little point.

(d) Are you wearing sensible garters or 'tie-ups'? Make sure that they are *not* too tight, but equally ensure that your socks do not keep slipping down. This can not only look sloppy, it also prevents you wearing shin pads and I would strongly recommend that you all wear something to guard your shins. Too many young players (and professionals) run the risk of receiving a nasty injury by not wearing them and I suggest that you will not only be better protected, but that you will have the confidence to go into the tackle more courageously if you wear the light, but effective modern shin-guard.

(e) Finally when you are looking the part, wearing your team kit,

[97]

clean boots and correct studs, make quite sure that your muscles are also ready for the game by warming up properly either in the changing room or on the pitch itself. There is nothing more frustrating than pulling a muscle in the first five minutes of the match, and remember on a cold day that it is often not a bad idea to apply some vaseline (or linament) on your exposed muscles before you venture forth.

(2) *A typical week in the life of a football professional*

Throughout this book I have been making constructive use of various photographs of Martin Dobson when he was at Everton, showing us how the basic techniques of the game can be mastered. Dobson is a fairly typical example of a good English professional – only briefly making the England team, but an important cog in Everton's footballing machine and a talented member of the promising young Burnley side for six years before that. His elegant style and his intelligent application have done much to contribute to the successes of both clubs while he was playing for them, and it says much for his loyalty that he should have returned to Burnley in 1979.

However, it is life off the field rather than on it, that I want to consider in this section. Before we analyse the professionals during the game itself, let us look with Dobson at his life behind the scenes. To start with it is important to realize that nowadays, after close-season tours and before pre-season practice matches that the professional only has five to six weeks' summer holiday between the football seasons. The only chance, apart from Sundays, to give full attention to the family – and to get away from football. Training for a new season usually starts in mid-July, initially geared to stamina, and probably involving both mornings and afternoons for the first three or four weeks. As matches start and the season progresses, naturally the training is not so intense and ball work replaces pure stamina work in most clubs. Dobson will normally train on Monday, Tuesday and Friday mornings during the winter months, probably playing a match on Wednesday as well as Saturday. Like many modern professionals he makes good use of his 'free afternoons'. It

[98]

95 Martin Dobson practising at his club training ground.

is true that a lot of time is spent travelling to and from away games and there is always golf to attract the energetic; but Dobson spends quite a lot of his spare time keeping in touch with the family firm, attending courses or studying at evening classes locally. Professional football is a young man's game and intelligent players like Martin Dobson realize the crucial need to look to a stable and assured future. Not everyone can become coach and manager; not everyone wants to!

Back to the professional's week. Everything is really geared towards the next match and if it is on a Saturday afternoon, this means a relatively early night on Thursday and Friday, a tactics talk on the Friday morning after the final light training session and on the Saturday a long lie-in and a sensible lunch before travelling to the ground in good time. On away games, the team usually travel on the Friday by train if they have a match in London, by coach otherwise, booking in to a hotel and having dinner together. On the Saturday the team would normally miss breakfast and enjoy a light protein lunch (fish or eggs) at 11.30. This would be followed by a final tactics talk and team discussion, when the manager would probably emphasize one or two points about the opposition and announce the starting line-up.

And so to the dressing room and the final preparations for the game itself. A cup of tea and a few firm words from the coach at half time and then it is all over – for better or for worse. A drink or two with the other players and then the journey home. Dobson lives 30 miles or so from his home ground and much enjoys 'escaping' from the public glare soon after a home game. Of course he, like any other good professional, realizes that he is bound to find intrusions on his private life, he signs autographs happily, opens fêtes and bazaars, talks to strangers, accepts the rough and the smooth from sports journalists. But he enjoys living in an area where he is not always recognized, and likes to get away from football and relax on a Saturday evening – particularly if he has had a bad game. Sometimes he will miss the Saturday night 'Match of the Day' on TV, preferring to join his wife and friends for a social evening. He also makes the relevant point that he does not worry so much now when the press or the TV commentators criticize his performance; but that young players often find it very difficult to adjust to the adulation of the press at one stage and their stinging criticisms at others. Equally Dobson reminds us that injuries are a worrying time for the professional, with frequent visits to the treatment room, advice from the physiotherapist and all the frustrations involved. Martin Dobson himself has been lucky in this respect and he is relieved too that he does not, like some professionals, have to watch his diet cautiously to keep his weight in check. He has obviously enjoyed his career as a professional footballer, giving much pleasure and gaining a lot too. It is a lucrative profession at the top level, a good First Division player might earn £10,000 a year – for 15 years if he remains fit and on top of his game; but Dobson reminds us that the family and the future are more important in the long run.

His final advice to any aspiring young player — by all means have a go at becoming a professional. It is a great life when all goes well; but remember that of thousands who try it only a handful reach the top of the tree.

(3) *Watching your team*

We all love to support 'our team' whether it be 'The United', 'The Rovers', 'The City', our local amateur team or even our School Eleven, and on these occasions we become so involved in the performance of our side, so worked up about the result that we often fail to learn anything from what we have seen. No doubt all of you, either with your father or a friend, have at some time or another been to watch a professional game, and no doubt you enjoyed the atmosphere, the excitement and the goals. But did you really learn anything worthwhile about the game? Did you watch the football intelligently? Or, like so many spectators nowadays, did you merely shout fanatically for your team and shout abuse at the opposition, the referee and the linesmen? Surely this is not the way to watch football! By all means enjoy yourself, get your money's worth, but make a point of learning from the experts. You will be surprised how much you can coach yourself and improve your football by intelligent watching.

You can either watch the general picture of play and appreciate a team's tactics, or, more profitably at your age, try watching a single player (preferably in your own position) for five to ten minutes with or without the ball. Bearing this in mind let us first look at:

THE GOALKEEPER

(a) Study that goalkeeper and notice how he is never still – even when play is at the other end of the field; look at the position he takes up as the opposing winger is about to centre; and see how far he is prepared to advance from his goal-line to help his defence.

(b) Analyse the goalkeeper's use of the ball. Is he throwing it quickly and accurately? Why is he kicking it high and hard – is it because his tall centre forward is waiting to head it on? Is he taking too long over those clearances? Why?

(c) How much is he talking to his defenders? Is he a calming in-fluence or merely spreading panic and concern?

THE DEFENCE

(a) Notice how coolly and sensibly professional defenders often play their way out of trouble. Look at the way they so often play the way they are facing – even if it is briefly backwards. Count the num-ber of wild clearances the full backs make in a game. You will be surprised how few there are.

(b) Frequently you will appreciate that a defence is not tackling, nor even marking very closely in midfield. Notice how a midfield player, if in doubt, will not rush into a tackle, but will back away 'containing' his opponent. But look at that mass of defenders guard-ing the penalty area. You will note that there is no 'holding off' or loose marking here in the danger zone! Look at that fierce tackling, and powerful heading that is so vital near goal. If you watch closely you will observe that the best defenders are 'man watchers' not 'ball watchers'. This means that although they have one eye on the ball, they watch the forward they are marking like a lynx, when he is near the danger area. What positions do the defenders take up at a corner? How does it differ from your corner drill? Are the full backs posi-tioned on the goal-line as in photograph **81**?

(c) Have you noticed, too, how often defenders normally pass the

96 Watch the professional goalkeeper carefully even when he is doing the simple things and learn from him. Ken Mulhearn in practice.

ball to a forward's feet, rather than in front of him? Take a closer look next time.

(d) Unfortunately there is usually such a noise at any professional match that you cannot hear the players, but they can hear each other and you might be amazed to realize just how much helpful talking does go on. If you watch carefully you can often see a forward warning his colleague of what is happening behind him. The shout of, 'Plenty of time, Mike', is much more valuable than, 'Give us a pass, Mike'. Do you shout helpfully in your team?

THE ATTACK

(a) One of the most instructive of all lessons to be learnt by watching a football match is that of movement 'off' the ball. Do you know the length of time an average player is in possession of the ball during a 90-minute game? Two minutes at the most! This means that for over 88 minutes we are playing football 'without the ball'! No wonder the best footballers in the world are those who play intelligently without the ball. Take a single player next time you watch and notice how he positions himself; where he runs; how he finds extra space for himself; when he sprints and how he rarely relaxes. How often for instance are you standing still on the left wing while the ball is with your right back? Watch the professional.

(b) Notice how professional footballers rarely run at one pace. Watch that sudden change of pace by a winger with the ball, or a centre forward without it. Do you change pace often in a game?

(c) How often have you come away from a game you have watched blaming perhaps the centre forward for having a bad game? But think back, wasn't it because the opposing defender marked him so well? Then there was that striker who scored three goals – most impressive, but how well was he marked?

(d) On other occasions you will have joined in the applause for a winger's rocket shot, which strikes the post from a very narrow angle; but if you have been looking closely you would have noticed that he had only to pass the ball gently back, and the centre forward was far better placed to shoot. You may also applaud a player who dribbles past five opponents; but did you notice the way in which he could have split the defence with a quicker pass to another of his forwards?

(e) Finally, you young forwards should note how often professional footballers are prepared to take a shot. One of the vivid lessons from the 1978 World Cup in Argentina lay in the remarkable number of goals scored from 30 metres or more. Do you remember Rep's goal against Scotland or Hahn's accurate long shots which helped to knock out the Germans and the Italians? We can all learn a lesson from this sort of shooting, so get practising and do not be frightened to 'have a go' from outside the penalty box.

GENERAL TACTICS

When you watch a game of football there are several other general points to note:

(a) When the professionals warm up before the game, notice how they split into small groups, not all shooting at the goalkeeper and how they stretch their muscles before the game starts. Do you give yourself time to warm up properly?

(b) Watch out for 4-2-4 or 4-3-3 or 4-4-2; the 'overlap'; the 'sweeper' and other methods. Notice how many teams recoil back into a packed defence and then suddenly spring out into counter-attack. Notice again how many teams claim most of the territorial advantage in a game and yet create fewer clear-cut scoring chances than the opposition. Why is this?

(c) What about the temperament of the players? Do you realize why some footballers play better in a crisis, whilst others become rattled and lose their tempers too easily? Self-discipline is of vital importance in football so take careful note!

(d) Look out for the 'offside trap'. Is it being operated effectively; or have the opposing team found a way to combat it? Remember that it only requires one defender to move out too slowly for the trap to fail.

(e) How many 'one touch' passing movements are attempted? One of the features of the modern game – underlined in Argentina – is the way in which South American and Continental teams seem to possess a more instinctive flair for 'one-touch' football. Do the teams you support ever string together five or more passes of this sort? If

[105]

they do, then the opposing defence should beware, because accurate one-touch football is quite unstoppable.

(f) Finally listen to the crowd's comments. Are they knowledge-able? All too rarely, you will discover. How often do you criticize a referee or linesman, when you are 100 metres away (or even watching the game on television); and he is on the spot – and fully qualified?

BEWARE

Finally a word of warning. Let us remember that professional foot-ball, while teaching us so many good points, can also teach us many undesirable features of the game. Sadly some of the greatest club teams are most to blame in this respect. What sort of things am I referring to?

(a) Unpleasant and unnecessary fouling.

(b) Objecting to a referee's decision. Of course he sometimes makes a mistake (he is only human) but throwing the ball away or swearing loudly will not help – and the odds are that he knows far more about the rules than you do. (Try being a referee yourself.)

(c) Time wasting. When money is involved this is perhaps under-standable (though never commendable) but certainly your game will prove more enjoyable for all concerned if you do not deliberately waste time.

(d) Appealing to the referee or linesman all the time. You will see the professional player doing far too much of this. Perhaps he is trying to put pressure on the officials, but do not bother to copy your hero in this respect. It does not help anybody in the end, all it does is lower your team's reputation for sportsmanship.

(e) Pretending to be badly hurt when you are not. Again this is not playing the game in the right spirit. Do not copy the professional player who puts on this sort of act.

(f) Hugging and kissing a goal scorer. There are always moments when one of our team scores a brilliant goal at a critical moment and instinctively we run to him and slap him on the back or shake his hand; such a reaction is only natural and no one can really object to this; but is there really any need to put on a display of exhibi-tionism whenever your team scores any goal? Does the mobbing and hugging of a footballer really help the image of soccer?

(g) Lastly you will see teams which play badly and are tactically unintelligent. Look out for this. Do not feel that the professional always knows more than you. In particular notice how many English teams resort to the long chip into the penalty area from all angles – regardless of the strength of their forwards in the air – when it would be far more effective to keep the ball on the ground.

(4) Analysing the great players

Once you have learned to prepare yourself fully for your own game and then started to watch the professionals more selectively, your performance will undoubtedly improve. But whether we are thinking of young musicians, young actors or young sportsmen, you will learn most of all by watching and studying the great artists. Therefore in this section I shall be analysing some of the outstanding footballers of the present decade. Cruyff of Holland, Keegan of England, Ardiles of Argentina and Beckenbauer of West Germany, four who have already earned a passport to greatness; and six on the verge of great things, Liam Brady of Eire, Viv Anderson and Peter Barnes of England, Paolo Rossi of Italy, Kenny Dalglish of Scotland and England's Trevor Francis. Naturally there are several brilliant players who are not included here, and, if I have omitted your particular hero, remember that I have not attempted to select an all-star XI. However, I am sure that no one will question the claim to fame of my first model.

(a) JOHANN CRUYFF

Although sadly he decided not to play in the 1978 World Cup, Johann Cruyff has established himself as one of the greatest European forwards ever to play the game. A combination of sharp intelligence and supreme skill made him, on his day, an impossible player to mark. Whether playing for Ajax of Amsterdam, the Dutch National team or his Spanish Club, Barcelona, Cruyff always had much to offer any student of the game. Like the great Pele he had complete mastery of the ball and possessed the same searing change of pace and like Beckenbauer, he roamed the football field with complete self-confidence. But what can you young players learn from him? Apart from the qualities that I have already mentioned, I suggest that there are two other outstanding characteristics of Cruyff's game. Firstly he was an imaginative, creative player who refused to be straight-jacketed into a narrow role. Not for him the predictable run or the coached, safety pass. Cruyff was always looking for the unexpected and quite prepared to wander out of position in order to avoid tight-marking. Remember that forwards who are unpredictable in their passing and running are far more difficult to mark. Secondly Cruyff was a brilliant tactician. Fully aware of the need to slow the game down on occasions and put his foot on the ball; yet brilliantly incisive when the opening presented itself. So many players, receiving the ball in midfield will automatically 'lay it off' or pass it back or square whether being marked or not. In such a situation Cruyff would turn and run explosively straight at (and often through!) the opposing defence. Of course Cruyff was able to give full expression to his creative abilities because he played in a Dutch team which believed in 'total football'. Those who saw Holland defeat the West Germans and the Italians in Argentina in 1978, or narrowly and perhaps un-luckily fail to win the World Cup in 1974, will remember the way defenders like Krol or Brandts would suddenly become attackers and how no Dutch player seemed to have a fixed position for long. I vividly recall seeing Cruyff and Holland give England a lesson in this flexible football at Wembley in 1976. They only won 2-0, but it is difficult to forget the worried looks on the faces of the English centre backs that day – Watson and Doyle – when they found no orthodox centre forward to mark. Instead they discovered the left back and then the opposing centre half coming at them! That is the way to play football – with flair, imagination and skill. That was Johann Cruyff's approach.

97 Johann Cruyff

(b) KEVIN KEEGAN

Whether playing for Liverpool, Hamburg or for England, Keegan has established himself as one of the outstanding players in World football today. He is at his best as a mobile front runner, not an orthodox winger, nor as a genuine centre forward, but playing off a big striker up front. When you next have the chance to watch Keegan, notice how difficult he is to mark closely. Many a defender has been detailed to mark him tightly and hopefully to play him out of the game; but this is easier said than done, due to his speed over 5 metres, his intelligent anticipation and his unpredictable running. Not for Keegan the obvious runs (back, forwards or sideways), when he is searching for a pass. No, he tends to leave his run as late as possible and then is always prepared to change direction at the last moment. In addition he will use the lateral (crossfield) run frequently, and he possesses the uncanny instinct of 'finding space' even against a packed defence. When Liverpool won the European Cup for the first time against Borussia Moenchengladbach, Bertie Vogts the experienced German international defender was given the job of tight-marking Keegan and found to his and his club's cost that it was virtually impossible. So if you want to learn how to play without the ball, watch Keegan – not on TV – but in the flesh.

However, he is an exciting footballer with the ball too and, though not an outstanding goalscorer, his darting runs around the edge of the penalty box provide numerous goals for others. He is a fine passer and a remarkably good header of the ball for one so small, while he is an elusive dribbler at times too. But it is his intelligence, his awareness of space and his ability to move fast at the right time that single him out as a great player – and, what is more, there is always a refreshing sparkle and sense of enjoyment about the way he plays his football.

98 Kevin Keegan

(C) OSVALDO ARDILES

Nobody outside Argentina had heard much about Osvaldo Ardiles until the 1978 World Cup; and when the home team started quite impressively, it was not immediately apparent that the hub of the Argentina side was this little man in midfield. Since then, of course, he has emerged as an outstanding creative player both for his country and for Tottenham Hotspur. Many cynics suggested that he would not be able to use his skill in the rough and tumble of English League football – not to mention the mud – but he soon proved them wrong. At the same time he underlined the fact that skill and intelligence will always succeed when applied on a football field.

What makes Ardiles one of the finest midfield players in the world today? Firstly his ability to control the ball, to kill it dead and to move with it seemingly tied to his bootlaces. His close control is immaculate, but notice how he does not indulge in skill for skill's sake. If necessary he will indeed hold the ball and beat an opponent or two, but he is always aware of the incisive early ball and like all great players he can pace a pass to perfection. Secondly he has vision. Ardiles does not often give the long 40-metre pass, but he sees an opening quicker than most and will either dart into it (with or without the ball) or will send his colleague into it with a perceptive early ball. Kempes and Luque of the Argentine and Taylor and Hoddle of Spurs have all prospered due to Ardiles' service from behind. Yet the final and most remarkable quality in his play, is the manner in which he shields the ball, retains control of it even against the fiercest challenge. When you next see him in action note how, despite his physique, he rides the tackle and holds off opponents, due to his per-fect balance and intelligent anticipation. He will give you an object lesson in how to screen the ball. When you watch someone like Ardiles play, or Keegan for that matter, you soon realize that a foot-balling brain more than compensates for lack of physique.

99 Osvaldo Ardiles

(d) FRANZ BECKENBAUER

Young defenders need look no further than the great German player, Franz Beckenbauer, for your model. First with Bayern Munich, then as Captain of the West German National team and finally with New York Cosmos in the N.A.S.L., he has established himself as one of the finest centre backs ever to play football. Unlike so many defenders Beckenbauer used his skill and positional sense more than physique and strength. He could tackle decisively enough when required, but like that other outstanding captain and cover centre back, Bobby Moore, Beckenbauer relied most upon perfect positioning, intelligent anticipation and shrewd interception. In addition he brought a calmness and assurance to any defence in which he played. So you aspiring defenders can certainly learn from Beckenbauer's defensive play: but you will learn even more if you ever watch him 'live' or on film, as a creative player. His greatness lies in his ability to use his skill with the ball, and whether we watch him delivering a quick, but imaginative 30-metre pass to a forward, or suddenly bursting through a midfield gap with the ball at his feet, or emerging from nowhere to make or score a goal, he has always been a wonderful reminder to defenders that they should attack as well as defend. Skilful, perceptive defenders are worth their weight in gold!

So much for our four established masters and I hope that even if you have not watched them play yet, you will find the chance of doing so in the future on film or television if not on the field itself. But my next six footballers are still climbing the ladder and although they may not reach the very top, each of them is well worth watching and analysing next time you have the chance to do so.

(e) LIAM BRADY

Like many of the outstanding creative footballers Brady is a slight, frail figure at first glance. But he has a thoughtful football brain, a magic left foot and a deceptive change of pace and for these reasons he is always well worth watching. One of the most important quali- ties for any midfield creative player is the ability to vary his passing, to produce the unexpected and keep the opposing defenders guessing

as to what might happen next. Thus Brady will sometimes play an early 30-metre through ball; next he will look for a short 'give and go', then perhaps he will stop and put his foot on the ball, 'screen' it and slow the game down; and, by contrast, he will then run fast at the opposing defence if the space presents itself. Watch him next time and learn from his skill with the ball *and* from his clever positioning without it.

(f) KENNY DALGLISH

When Dalglish replaced Kevin Keegan in the Liverpool team at the start of the 1977–78 season, he seemed to be faced with an impossible task, stepping into the shoes (or boots) of his brilliant predecessor. Yet in a very different way, Dalglish has already proved himself to be an equally outstanding forward. Perhaps the most priceless skill he possesses is an ability to turn with the ball in tight situations, and it is this quality that has destroyed many 'tight-marking' centre

101 Kenny Dalglish

halves in their own penalty area and brought Dalglish numerous fine goals for Liverpool and Scotland. He is not a notable header of the ball, but has an even greater instinct for goals than Kevin Keegan. This is partly due to his anticipation and speed off the mark. Like many great players he is not very fast over 50 metres but looks extremely quick over the crucial first five. He also possesses that other vital asset in any goalscorer – courage. Yet like many other talented forwards, Dalglish must be used properly as Scotland found to their cost in the 1978 World Cup series. He needs the space that Liverpool's 4–4–2 system gives him and wants the ball passed to his feet rather than playing alongside a big, central striker as Scotland asked him to do in their 1978 World Cup debacle. Next time you have the chance to watch Dalglish in action, note particularly how cleverly he moves in his opponent's penalty area and how difficult he therefore is to mark.

(g) TREVOR FRANCIS

It is not easy to be labelled 'the first million pound footballer', but Trevor Francis has had to play with that particular millstone round his neck since being transferred from Birmingham City to Nottingham Forest in 1979. Naturally he took a little time to settle with his new club, but outstanding footballers soon adjust to different tactics and new team mates and Francis is no exception as he showed with a brilliant performance in the European Cup Final against Malmo. Like Dalglish he is a striker of rare quality. He relies also upon skill and intelligence rather than size and strength in the air, which has been the hallmark of so many centre forwards recently – particularly in England. Whether playing for Birmingham City and Nottingham Forest in England or for Detroit Express in the North American Soccer League, Trevor Francis possesses many of the attributes which young footballers should be striving to learn – intelligent running 'off the ball', sharp control, the ability to turn quickly in tight situations and an eye for goal which so often takes opposing defenders by surprise. Not for Francis the shelving of responsibility. If he sees the chance to run at his opposing defender he is quite prepared to dribble round him. Are you? If he sees half a shooting chance near goal he will 'have a go'. Do you?

(h) PAOLO ROSSI

Just as English soccer is always full of courage, discipline and stamina and the Argentinians at best a happy mixture of aggression and pure skill, so the Italians seem to produce on the one hand defenders totally dedicated to marking tight and tackling hard, while developing attackers full of grace and elegance. Bettega was such a player but the young centre forward Rossi is perhaps worth a particularly close study. You may have seen him playing in the 1978 World Cup or since then for Italy and one of the first things that will strike you young players is the deceptively casual way in which he moves. It is always a sign of class, if a footballer seems to have plenty of time and Rossi gives this impression. Why is this? Partly, I suggest because of his long-legged build, but more important, because he is intelligent enough to anticipate a move or a pass *before* his marker and because, when the ball arrives, he possesses the confident close control which all great centre forwards need. Next time you find the chance to watch him in action notice especially those little 10-metre angled runs he makes either side of the opposing centre half, often taking up unexpected positions to help his colleagues. Not for Rossi the big thundering burst through the middle or the old fashioned physical challenge. He is tough enough and he scores a lot of fine goals, but he glides onto the through ball and uses skill rather than brawn to create himself a shooting chance in the penalty box. Obviously it depends greatly upon what system your team is playing, but if you are a budding centre forward I suggest that you can probably learn as much from Rossi as from any other central striker playing today.

(i) VIVIAN ANDERSON

One of the exciting developments in football during the last ten years has been the emergence of the game amongst Africans, West Indians and in the Middle East. Anyone who saw the Iran and Tunisian teams in the 1978 World Cup will have noted the significant strides that have recently been made in these areas; and talented players such as Cyrille Regis, Laurie Cunningham and Viv Anderson in the English First Division further emphasize the breakthrough made in the 1970's by black British footballers.

I have chosen Viv Anderson as the one to study, partly because he was the first coloured player to win a full England Cap and partly because he is an outstanding example of the attacking full back. All defenders, as we have previously noted, must first and foremost know how to mark, to tackle and to stop opposing forwards. Anderson's long-legged tackling, his shrewd positional sense and his height and strength in the air enable him to carry out his defensive duties effectively. But his greatest quality lies in his attack. His confidence with the ball and his willingness to come forward in support of his forwards are object lessons to any young full back. There are other outstanding defenders who pass the ball more imaginatively than Anderson, but there are very few (if any) who surge through so decisively with the ball at their feet. Next time you have the chance to watch him, see how positively he overlaps, how aggressively he is prepared to take opponents on and have a shot at goal if the opportunity arises. But watch too, for the alert manner in which he recovers fast if the attack breaks down, and marks his opposing winger as quickly as possible.

(j) PETER BARNES

Wing play seemed to be a dying art a few years ago, but the emergence of young wingers like Barnes have stirred memories of famous predecessors such as Matthews and Finney of England, Gento of Spain or Garrincha of Brazil. Barnes is blessed with those priceless qualities of speed and dribbling skill which are so important to a winger. Watch the way that he is prepared to go past his full back on the inside and on the outside. Note how close he takes the ball to his opponent before accelerating past him and look carefully too, at the perfect balance required by a top class dribbler. Wingers, like central strikers, need courage too — the nerve to run at hard tackling defenders and to come back for more after a fierce challenge. Finally note how wingers of Barnes's quality are two footed, able to switch to either flank and how the great winger does not just beat his full back with a clever dummy or change of speed – but then crosses the ball accurately too. Do you?

102 Peter Barnes

(5) *A Closer look at a Great Team*

Wherever you live and whatever team you support, if you know any-thing at all about football, you will have to agree that Liverpool are one of the finest club sides in the world today. They have won the English First Division title 11 times in all, on four occasions between 1972 and 1979 when they never finished lower than third in the table. They have also won the F.A. Cup twice and have achieved the re-markable feat of qualifying for Europe in every season since 1963. More recently, of course, they have won the final of the highly-prized European Cup in consecutive seasons, defeating Borussia 3–1 in 1977 and then beating Bruges, the Belgium champions, more easily than the 1–0 score suggested in 1978. A magnificent record of consistency. Perhaps it is the loyal supporters, or perhaps the club's knack of blending the best of Irish, Scottish, Welsh and English players into a team, or just the guiding genius of Bill Shankley and Bob Paisley, the two managers who have shared such regular triumphs – whatever the reason for success, we can all learn by a closer analysis of Liverpool's style of play.

Most of you will have watched Liverpool play either in live action or on television, but I wonder if you have really appreciated the underlying qualities in their team. I suggest that next time you have the good fortune to watch them, you note the following 10 outstand-ing characteristics:

1. *Team spirit:* This might seem an old fashioned term these days, but it is still vital to a successful side and Liverpool have it in abun-dance. Notice the way they play *for each other*, how they run for each other and how they cover for a team-mate who is having a poor game.

2. *Resilience and character:* Qualities that go towards team spirit. Liverpool sometimes have an 'off day' and things naturally go wrong on occasions, but if Liverpool fall behind you do not see any heads dropping and shoulders drooping. You see Hughes clapping his hands, Clemence clenching his fist and within no time they are on level terms. There are skilful 'prima donnas' in other club sides; but not at Liverpool. Even the most gifted ball players have to work and work again – as Callaghan and Sounness have proved.

3. *Confidence:* This is an intangible quality, but Liverpool players all possess it, because they have confidence in each other. Look at the way they take opposing players on, whether it is forwards like

Heighway, Keegan or defenders like Alan Kennedy or Hughes. Equally note the fact that Liverpool players never seem afraid to take the responsibility of having a shot. We have seen splendid goals by defenders, Smith, Neal and Thompson, but particularly impressive has been the powerful and confident shooting from mid-field. Jimmy Case, Ray Kennedy and Terry McDermott have all scored spectacular goals from outside the penalty box when lesser sides would be thinking of passing the ball square instead.

4. *Strength in depth:* Another of Liverpool's qualities. Any successful club side nowadays needs a squad of 15–16 players to cover for injuries or loss of form and Liverpool are well equipped in this respect. Their reserve team more than often finishes top of the table of their particular league and fine players like Johnson, Fairclough and Hanson underline their powerful reserve strength. It says much for Liverpool that they are able to keep such talented players when they could find regular first team football with most other professional clubs.

5. *Players complement each other:* There is no weak link in the Liverpool team, and that can be confidently said over the past 15 years. Equally, although there have been international stars, such as Keegan, Clemence, Heighway, Dalglish, etc., it has never been a matter of relying upon three or four gifted individuals. Any successful team needs players who complement each other, as Roger Hunt and Ian St John, Kevin Keegan and John Toshack for instance. In today's team that balance is still very apparent – particularly in midfield, always the heart of any Liverpool side. Note how Terry McDermott supplies the non-stop running and the defensive tackling, how Ray Kennedy provides the shooting and heading power and the calmness, how Graham Sounness has added the creative skill and the imagination and Jimmy Case the width, strength and speed. Has your team found this balance?

6. *Patience:* Another of Liverpool's qualities is patience, particularly when opposed to defensive tactics by their opponents. Next time you watch them, note how often they hold the ball in midfield, pass back, keep possession waiting for the opening to appear. Liverpool are masters of this game of chess.

7. *Strength in the tackle:* You rarely see Liverpool players losing the

ball in the tackle. This is particularly true of defenders like Tommy Smith or Phil Thompson but when watching Liverpool notice how Jimmy Case, Steve Heighway and other forwards tackle back so determinedly.

8. *Speed:* Although the Liverpool team includes players who are not all that quick, one of the features of their game is speed. This is particularly noticeable against foreign opposition in the various European competitions when they refuse to slow their pace to suit opponents. Players like Keegan, Callaghan, Heighway, Fairclough, Case and Dalglish epitomize Liverpool's emphasis on speed. Nor is there any special preoccupation with the short game. To use an old-fashioned phrase they believe still in 'swinging it about' – quickly!

9. *Width:* Many teams playing 4-4-2 or 4-3-3 (which are Liverpool's usual permutations) tend to neglect the touchlines and make it easy for opposing defenders by crowding into the middle. Not so Liverpool. They often play one winger – Fairclough or Heighway – but notice how wide he stands and if he is not out on the touchline Phil Neal from full back or Jimmy Case or Ray Kennedy from midfield are soon filling the space there and stretching the opposing defence. Good tactics; and watch too how Liverpool so often aim to get behind defenders and to reach the bye-line – such a dangerous threat to any defence.

10. *No soft goals:* Partly because of the calibre of a goalkeeper like Ray Clemence, but partly because of the strict discipline and understanding in the Liverpool defence, we rarely see them give away a 'soft goal'. Yet how frequently other teams (yes, professional ones too) make that vital casual error in their own penalty area? If there is any real threat you will see Liverpool defenders banging the ball out of the 'danger area' as quickly as possible. Take note. Do not try to play too much pretty football immediately in front of your own goalmouth.

Liverpool may not be the most exciting team to watch; there are plenty of sides with more gifted individuals, others that score more imaginative goals, but as *a team* they are second to none. We can learn a lot by watching them carefully even if they are playing against our favourite team. So next time you are lucky enough to see them play, remember my ten points.

[122]

CHAPTER 10

Some Important Laws of the Game

It is amazing in these days when football is such a popular game and millions of people play and watch matches at all levels, that so many players and even more spectators do not really understand the laws themselves. How many times have you seen a referee or linesman's decision questioned by supporters at the other end of the ground, or by players a long way from the scene of the incident? All too often. How many times have you fallen into the modern habit of questioning or appealing to the referee? Too often again, I suspect. Obviously referees and linesmen make mistakes and the slow motion replay on television is sometimes a cruel reminder of this. But, whether he is right or wrong, the referee's decision *is* final and the sooner you accept that and get on with the game, the sooner you will be playing the game in the right spirit.

You will also appreciate the referee's decisions more fully and play the game more effectively if you really know the rules. I do not intend to list all the laws of the game here but it might be helpful to look at some of the more troublesome ones.

LAW 1. *The Size of the Pitch*
This law gives all the information about the field of play, its dimensions and the method of marking out goal area, penalty area, etc. The key point here is that the touch-lines and goal-lines *are* part of the field of play – whereas in Rugby football they are not. Goalkeepers are reminded under Law 1 that they can be penalized for misconduct if, in an effort to save a shot, they seize hold of the crossbar and pull it down. So you tall young keepers be warned!

LAW 2. *The Ball*

Only the referee can authorize the changing of a ball during the game, however much you blame it for your poor play!

LAW 3. *Substitutes*

Remember that, if you are the substitute, you must wait for the referee to call you on to the field of play and should inform him of your name or number.

LAW 4. *Players Equipment*

One of the important points to remember here concerns your studs. They must not be dangerous and it is always worth checking your boots carefully (and cleaning them of course) before any game.

Do not forget, too, that the referee is entirely within his rights in ordering you to take off a watch or a bracelet or pendant if he considers that they might cause danger to other players.

LAWS 5 AND 6 concern the referee and linesman specifically.

LAW 7. *The duration of the game*

The official length of the game is ninety minutes, but this may be shortened by mutual agreement in exceptional circumstances. However, for most boys 40 minutes each way is usual and for Under 14 teams 30 minutes each way is ample – particularly on muddy, heavy pitches.

LAW 8. *The Kick Off*

Two points need remembering here. Firstly you must not cross the half-way line, nor must opponents enter the centre-circle *until* the ball has been kicked. You must not move on the whistle, but after the first kick. Secondly the ball must go forward and roll a full circumference before it is in play and before another player may touch it.

LAW 9. *Ball in and out of play*

(a) The ball is out of play when it has *wholly* crossed the goal-line or touch-line, whether on the ground or in the air. Furthermore a player in touch may continue to play a ball not wholly off the field of play.

(b) The ball is also out of play when the game has been stopped by the referee. The ball is in play at all other times from the start of the game to the finish.

Remember that it is entirely up to the referee as to how much 'injury time' be added on at the end of a game and he can equally decide whether or not to add on further seconds for time-wasting! It is also worth bearing in mind that if the ball strikes the referee while he is on the field of play the game continues.

LAW 10. *The Scoring of a Goal*
Again we find that the 'whole of the ball must cross the goal-line, between the goal-posts and under the bar. It must not have been thrown, knocked-on, nor carried there by any players of the attacking side'. It is possible, therefore, for the goalkeeper to have his feet behind the line when catching the ball: on the other hand, if he stands in front of the line, but in drawing his arm back to throw the ball clear, the ball crosses the line – it is a goal!

The referee sometimes has a very difficult decision to make when the ball strikes the underside of the crossbar and bounces downwards. The ball is usually spinning and the only two people who are really in position to know whether it is a goal or not are the linesman and the goalkeeper (who is probably flat on his face anyway!). In this respect, you might have seen film of the memorable but controversial goal scored by Hurst for England against West Germany in the World Cup Final of 1966.

LAW 11. *Off-side*
The interpretation of this law produces more argument and discord in football than any other, but the law itself is quite clear. It reads, 'A player is off-side if he is nearer his opponents' goal-line than the ball at the moment the ball is played, unless:

(a) He is in his own half of the field of play.

(b) There are two of his opponents nearer to their own goal-line than he is.

(c) The ball last touched an opponent or was last played by him.' The vital words here are *'at the moment the ball is played'*. A player can run 10 to 20 metres while the ball is in the air, after it has been kicked and will often appear to be a long way off-side when he collects the pass, yet probably is not. This is why it is very dangerous to try to play the 'off-side game', quite apart from the poor spectacle it presents to spectators.

It is also important to realize that you cannot be off-side at a goal-kick, corner, throw-in or when the ball is dropped by the referee. Nor are you infringing the rule if you are standing a good 15 metres off-side when you intercept a pass back from one of your opponents intended for the goalkeeper. So you defenders must always make sure before you pass back to your keeper!

Finally never forget to play to the whistle – particularly where off-sides are concerned. If you are a defender it is no good appealing, or standing waiting for a decision in your favour. Get on with the game and leave the judgement to the one man who can see an off-side most clearly – the linesman.

LAW 12. (a) *Fouls*

'A player shall be penalized if he *intentionally*:

1   Kicks, strikes or jumps at an opponent.
2   Trips an opponent.
3   Handles the ball.
4   Holds or pushes an opponent.
5   Charges in a violent or dangerous manner; or charges an opponent from behind unless the latter be obstructing.'

I quote these extracts from the Law to show that infringements under these headings must be *intentional* before a foul is committed. It is important to remember that football is partly a physical contest and it would be a sad day if we eliminated all bodily contact from the game. A good, clean charge, or a hard but fair tackle is infinitely preferable to the ankle tapping, shirt tugging, or kicking over the ball (that we see too often today) as a method of stopping an opponent.

(b) *Misconduct*

In addition to the fouls listed above, do not forget that you can be penalized for *dangerous play* and *ungentlemanly conduct*. These cover a wide variety of sins, ranging from 'studs up', swinging your boot too high, showing dissent, swearing and even playing without any shorts on! These offences might well lead to your being shown the yellow card (a warning) or even a red card (being sent off) but along with obstruction – often a difficult law to implement – they can both be penalized by an indirect free kick rather than a direct one. It is worth recalling here that the referee should always indicate an indirect free kick by raising one arm high above his head – otherwise you know that it is direct. Some referees are stricter than others in applying this rule, but it is up to you to ensure that you know what is a foul and what is not, and to accept the fact that even the best referee in the world cannot see everything – until he watches the action replay on TV the following day!

(c) *Goalkeepers*

Law 12 also reminds you goalkeepers that you are only allowed four steps before releasing the ball. An indirect free kick is the punishment. A goalkeeper must be carrying the ball before he can be charged in his goal area and then squarely (shoulder to shoulder) but outside it he becomes an ordinary player and can be charged if within playing distance of the ball.

In reality, however, goalkeepers are usually given much more protection than this, especially in the professional ranks. But do remember that if you are charged by the centre forward while you hold the ball, you are *not* allowed to charge him back.

LAW 13. *Free Kick*

'When a free kick is being taken, a player of the opposite side shall not approach within 10 yards of the ball until it is in play, unless he is standing on his own goal-line between the posts.'

This speaks for itself; but do not forget that a good referee will often play the 'advantage rule' even if you have been fouled.

LAW 14. *The Penalty Kick*

There are several points to note here. Firstly the goalkeeper should stand without moving his feet on his own goal line until the ball has been kicked. Secondly the ball must not be played by the kicker a second time until it has been touched by another player. Thus, if the ball rebounds from the bar or the post you may not play it again; but if the goalkeeper has touched your shot onto the bar or post and it rebounds back to you, think yourself lucky and thump it into the net!

LAW 15. *Throwing*

'The thrower at the moment of delivering the ball must face the field of play and part of each foot shall be either on or outside the touch line.'

So you can take a quick throw from say 5 metres outside the field of play and you can stand with one foot in front of the other.

'The thrower shall use both his hands and shall deliver the ball from behind and over his head.'

This reminds us that the ball must be thrown and not just dropped and that a one-handed throw is not allowed. Practise your throwing, because all members of the side (except the keeper) will need to know how to throw and it is remarkable how many boys do not know this particular rule.

LAW 16. *The Goal Kick*

This can be taken anywhere inside the six-yard area as long as it is in the same half nearest to the point where the ball went over the goal-line. Remember, too, that if the goal kick does not reach the edge of the penalty area, or touches another player before it does so, the kick must be retaken. You will not have forgotten, I hope, what the law says about the goal kick which is blown back into your own goal?

LAW 17. *Corner Kick*

This law is fairly straightforward but remember that you are not allowed to remove the corner flag while you are taking the kick.

I hope that this survey of the laws will help all young footballers to enjoy the game more fully and assist all budding referees too. Equally I hope that the advice and the coaching offered in this short book will enable you to make the most of your ability and to enjoy more completely the greatest game on earth. For when all is said and done few games can compete with the great combination of skill and stamina, imagination and discipline that soccer offers. Those of us who have played it, coached it and watched it have gained an enormous amount of enjoyment and made numerous lasting friendships. The more we know the game, the greater its rewards.